Five
OUT
OF
Eleven

LeTicia Rivera-Clemente

Published with support from
LWI Publishing Services

Printed in the United States of America
First Printing: October 2025

ISBN: 979-8-9999453-0-3

"The key in all of this is to truly lean in as you let go and let God."

DEDICATION

*To all of my children lost and living, without you none of this would be possible and I don't know who or where I'd be without you. And to my husband, thank you for always supporting me in everything I do and have ever done.
I love you.*

CONTENTS

Dedication

Prologue 1

1 October 7, 2005 3

2 Ariah 15

3 The Wedding 31

4 Emergency 45

5 What Next? 55

6 Azriel 69

7 Methotrexate 89

8 Aaliayh 103

9 Adrian 127

10 The 6th 147

11 Amir 157

12 Epilogue: The Blessing in it All 181

About the Author 187

Prologue

Faith was instilled in me at an early age and when I was seven, I made the decision to be baptized. Something, or should I say the Holy Spirit, spoke to my heart. I know what you're thinking. How could you know what you wanted or felt at the age of seven, you were persuaded, right? I wasn't. I can't explain it. I just knew the feeling I felt when I was in church and heard the choir sing beautiful songs of praise. That feeling of warmth I felt while I sat on the blue itchy pew and listened intently on what the Pastor was saying. Back then all I knew was that I wanted to feel that feeling of joy, and contentment all the time. But sometimes, that is impossible.

Highs and lows, happiness and sadness are a part of life. Pain and suffering are a natural part of life but is losing a child "natural"? How often do you ask, "Why is this happening?" or "Why me?" or

"Why can't I, get pregnant?" These are questions I asked myself often after having miscarriage after miscarriage. Questions many of you may have asked as well. I had so many questions and no answers. I questioned God, but not in a "how could you?" kind of way. I questioned Him in a confused, boggled sort of way and I wanted answers. I sought answers in places, and from people who could not give me the answers I wanted or needed. For me, getting pregnant was an amazing miracle that I did not take for granted, but the loss was catastrophic. And not just one loss.

CHAPTER 1

October 7, 2005

This can't be happening to me, and on my birthday of all days. There I was lying on an operating table, in a tiny room where small office procedures are done, cold and terrified. "I'm going to give you something that will help you relax and to keep you from remembering what's happening" the doctor said. *Keep me from remembering?* I thought. "There is nothing you can give me to make me forget this day" I said to myself. My grandmother was there in the room with me while my boyfriend waited in the designated waiting area. I remember hearing myself sob the whole time while my grandmother kept telling me that everything was going to be ok. But it was not ok, because I just had a D & C (Dilation and curettage). The procedure had to be done because I had a miscarriage. Little did I know that wouldn't be my last.

I was exactly 12 weeks pregnant when I went to the doctor for a sonogram to check on my baby. It was then that we, the sonographer and I, discovered that there was no heartbeat. The sonographer looked around my womb a little more than confirmed what I could already see on the monitor. "I'm sorry, there is no heartbeat," she said. She then told me that the doctor would go over the results of my sono with me and directed me to the room where I had to wait for my obstetrician (OB) to come in.

I absolutely loved my OB. She was the same physician who delivered my first child in 2002. She was very caring and thoughtful with her words. Sorrow led as she walked into the room to greet me. She told me she reviewed the sonographer's report and confirmed again that the heart was no longer beating. "I'm sorry LeTicia," she said. I just sat there and thought, *But I was just here four weeks ago and there was a heartbeat, the OB and I had heard it together.* "What do you mean there is no heartbeat, and what happened?" I asked. I didn't really know what to say or what to ask, or even what to expect.

4

My doctor's eyes were so kind, her voice was calm and helped keep me at ease, even though my emotions were in turmoil. "This happens sometimes, more than you realize," she said, "It wasn't anything you did wrong, these things just happen." As if that was supposed to make me feel better. She went on to explain that sometimes chromosomal abnormalities or other factors could be the cause. It was then that the room faded to black, and her words were no longer clear or comprehensible, you know, like in that cartoon with the teacher who you can't understand because the words are inaudible and sound like the repeated blaring of a trombone. I don't remember speaking after her explanation and I don't even remember getting off the table or walking down the hall to schedule my next appointment for the D&C. One thing I will never forget about that day is that once the appointment was made, I was told I would need to wait 2 days before the doctor could go in and remove the baby.

It was difficult waiting two whole days until the D&C appointment. My mind was never at rest and my body did not get much rest either. All I could think about were the what-ifs and why's. I thought about what they would do during the procedure and how it would feel, and how this birthday would be like no other.

Two days later I arrived at the appointment, and I was numb. My grandmother was with me holding my hand every step of the way. It all felt like a blurred bad dream, but I can remember when the doctor read the consent forms. It was at that moment that it all felt real. The paperwork stated that I was getting an abortion, but I never wanted an abortion. I just wanted my baby. I asked her why they used the word abortion, and her explanation was since they had to remove the baby, the procedure was considered an abortion. My first thought was *who came up with that stupid shit?* I didn't choose to have a miscarriage let alone an abortion. This was not deliberate. I wanted my baby. I did not want to have the procedure done.

To add insult to injury the doctor explained that insurance may not cover it. The doctor also went on to explain the anesthesia that I would be under and how I would not feel any pain and may not have any memory of the procedure. She explained how I would be awake through the entire procedure and that it would take less than twenty minutes to complete. Once the procedure was over, I would be left to lie there for another twenty to thirty minutes to allow the anesthesia to wear off a bit and once it did, I would be able to get up to walk out normally. Her last words being, "You may not have any memory of the procedure." *Well, that's a lie* I thought. I knew that wasn't true and that I would remember everything.

I remember lying there in that cold room crying as my grandmother held my hand. I cried the entire time and was crying out "Why?" loudly. As I play it back in my mind, it's like a scene in a movie where a woman is wailing, and you think as the viewer *she's being dramatic.* The doctor probably thought I was being dramatic, maybe because it's something she dealt with on a regular basis, but this was all new to me. To her it was probably just another "aborted fetus". Even though playing the scene back in my mind seems dramatic, it was not. I was overly emotional and had every right to be. It was heartbreaking and traumatic to say the least. I did not want to be there, I did not want to have a D&C, and I damn sure did not want to be having a D&C on my birthday.

Right after the doctor said she was done; I remember asking if I could see the baby. She looked a little confused and told me there was nothing to see but bloody tissue, but I still wanted to see. The fetus could have only been the size of a blueberry, or maybe a raspberry, or even the size of a green olive, but it was hard to say not knowing exactly when the heart and the growth stopped. I just wanted to see what the baby, my baby, looked like at that stage, for closure I guess, but there was no closure. The doctor held open a gauze like cloth with what looked to be bloody tissue and blood clots. It did not look like a baby, but I knew my baby was there, lifeless. At this point, I just wanted to get out of there, go get my daughter, and go home.

When I arrived home later that day, my mind was racing with thoughts of guilt, anger, anxiety, and tons of questions with no answers. The only answer I did have is that God knows best, and it just wasn't my time to have another child. Had it been a successful pregnancy, my oldest, Ariah, who was 3 at the time would have had a little brother or sister. I wanted that so bad for her. I didn't want her to be the only child or end up being more than 5 or more years apart from her siblings like I am. But God had other plans.

"I'm sorry you had to go through that" Adrian said quietly while we were in the car heading to dinner. He held my hand tight with his right hand while steering with his left, often looking over to me with compassion in his eyes and concern for my feelings there in his expression.

At the time, Adrian and I were engaged. We'd been together off and on for a total of five years when he finally proposed. "Try not to stress and let's try to enjoy the rest of your day" he said. *Well, that's easier said than done,* I thought. It was also like the doctor saying to me after the procedure that "I would just need to rest for a day or two and I'd be fine." I wasn't fine with any of what had happened, and I really did not want to go on with our original plans to go out for a birthday dinner. Without knowing this would be a day of disappointment, he previously made arrangements to take me to a little Italian place we both liked. Adrian knew the manager and reserved a private booth for us in the back of the restaurant where there were not many people. Once we were seated, we sat close to each other in the curve of an overly large U-shaped booth. We looked over the menu and called out all the entrées that sounded good to us as we waited for someone to come take our orders.

While we ate, I was not the chatty Cathy I usually am. We had moments of admiring the photographs and old-world Italian décor that embellished the room. We tried our best not to think about the loss we had just endured, and, at that moment, we did not talk much about what took place. In the quiet moments, my mind wandered off and everything in me wanted answers so of course I began to question myself again. "What did I do, what didn't I do, was it something I ate or maybe that drink I consumed before I knew I was pregnant." I thought about everything I could have done wrong and wracked my brain thinking of how I spent my last few weeks thinking it had to be something I did, and I blamed myself. Adrian could tell I was in my thoughts, and he put his arm around me as I sat there chewing with tears streaming down my face. Words weren't needed in that moment.

Over the next few weeks, I barely slept. There were many nights I lay awake just staring at the ceiling thinking about the child I had lost. Many of those nights I'd rub my stomach while imagining the movement I would have felt and the growth of my belly that would have occurred. I thought about how my body would have changed and wondered if it would have been the same as it was with my first child. Then like a train passing, all the negative thoughts came rushing in a flash, *Was I not going to church enough? Is it because I'm not married yet?*

Maybe I need to work out more, or eat better, or maybe there is something wrong with my body, or with my uterus. "Lord, what could it be?" I'd ask a thousand times. You can drive yourself crazy wondering about all the why's and what-ifs. Several months went by and I finally got to a place where I stopped asking God and myself why. I didn't talk about it much and I focused on the daughter I already had. There was still fear that this could happen to me again but my prayer to God was that it wouldn't. At that point, all I could do was put my trust in Him and take it one day at a time with the hopes that He would bless me with another child one day.

Trust in the Lord with all your heart and lean not on your own understanding; in all your ways submit to him, and he will make your paths straight.

Proverbs 3:5-6 NIV

CHAPTER 2

Ariah

I would have to say bringing Ariah into this world was easier than I thought it would be. The morning sickness I had was pretty normal and got a lot better after my 1st trimester ended. It mostly hit me in the mornings while preparing for work or just before I would eat breakfast and with an empty stomach it was mostly bile and dry heaving.

The worst part of being sick during that time was that I had to keep a cup in the car with me because of the nausea. It never failed, every time I passed a big truck with the smell of exhaust fumes vomiting was imminent. Among all the pregnancy symptoms I could have, I was thankful that I was not having back pain, but I had the weirdest black spots develop on both sides of my hips that made me look like a cheetah.

Adrian and I had been together for a year, but I was still unsure if he was who I wanted to be with at the time and if our relationship would turn into something long term. When we found out I was pregnant, we were both living with our grandparents, so it just made sense for us to get an apartment together. We both agreed it would be best for our child to have both parents in one place and for the most part, we enjoyed the apartment we shared together and did our best to make it a home, but there were days I couldn't stand to look at him or be around him and, in my mind, I had called it quits, but most of it was the pregnancy talking.

My favorite room in our apartment would become my daughter's nursery which was the second bedroom. One of the best parts of preparing the nursery was being able to creatively come up with the design with my childhood bestie who would become my sister-in-law. We had known each other since kindergarten. Who would have thought we would reconnect because we were dating brothers?

I had chosen a theme that was popular at the

time called Suzy's Zoo. Some of you may not know what that was or is, but it was the cutest neutral and gender friendly theme. We were so creative and visited craft stores and a huge teacher supply store to get supplies we needed, including lots of butcher paper, you know the kind on the huge rolls that you may see at schools. We created a large tree in the corner of the room with a swing hanging from one of the branches. We found large card stock character print outs to incorporate into the design and sat one of the large characters on the swing and placed the others throughout. We used large poly-fil, or cotton stuffing to create clouds on the walls since I couldn't paint the apartment. We used the large light blue sheets of butcher paper to cover the top part of the walls to look like the sky. The room was magical, and I knew my baby would love it just as much as we did.

I'd have to say my first pregnancy was my best pregnancy and surprisingly my labor was not at all what I expected or what everyone warned me about for my first child. Finally, the time was drawing near for me to meet my little girl who we decided to name Ariah. I got her name from a customer that had come through my line while working as a cashier during my part-time stint at Wal-Mart. A lady had the cutest little baby in the car seat of her basket, and I had to know what her name was, and she told me "Ariah." It was the best "A" name I'd heard, and I knew that was it. Adrian liked it also and we decided we would name our first daughter Ariah and let all our kids' names start with the letter "A."

We had talked about how many children we wanted on numerous occasions and Adrian told me that he wanted to have seven children. I always thought I'd be okay with having three or four, but I was actually good with that number and responded, "I would have however many God would allow". I believed the choice wasn't completely up to me. I could say I wanted to have three or seven but didn't know at the time what would be physically possible for me and my body so the best answer for me to give was however many God would allow.

While moonlighting at Wal-Mart, I was also

working a full-time job for the State of Texas at the time. The further along I got, the harder it became to go into work. Every time I had to leave work for a doctor's appointment I was hoping and praying my doctor would tell me I'm dilated enough, which would be at least two centimeters for them to keep me and admit me to the hospital. I think that's every woman's hope near the end of pregnancy. My belly had become so large that it was physically impossible to do many things like tie my shoe for instance, and it was becoming tiring getting in and out of my small Honda civic and to walk up and down the stairs to our apartment, so I was beyond ready for our baby to get here.

Although I had no complications during my first pregnancy, the doctor told me since I was nearing my 39th week she could schedule me for induction. I was excited about that because I could start my maternity leave a little sooner and I felt it gave me the time I needed to prepare for Ariah's arrival. However, the night before my scheduled induction, pain woke me from my sleep. Not that I was sleeping well in the first place. When was the last time you heard of a pregnant woman sleeping comfortably in her 9th month? My anxiety kept me tossing and turning most of the night as I anticipated the events to take place the next morning.

I was scheduled to go into the hospital at 6:30 the morning of June 19, 2002, for an induction, little did I know I'd begun to go into labor overnight. The pain that woke me was like a tightening in my belly, like someone was wringing out a towel known as my cervix. Were these contractions? I felt an intense amount of pressure as I inched to the bathroom that was only 4ft. away from my bed. After slowly lowering myself onto the toilet, I grabbed some toilet paper after peeing and noticed I had some mucus tinged with blood on the tissue. It was a habit I had, checking after every wipe for any indicators of losing my mucus plug. I carefully rose from the seated position to waddle to the sink to wash my hands and shuffled back to the nightstand on my side of the bed. I immediately called the nurse, waited on hold for about 5 minutes then explained to the woman on the other end of the phone what I was experiencing. She said it sounded like I was in labor and asked how far apart I thought the contractions were. I told her I'd felt discomfort all through the night, but the pain had just recently intensified and so I wasn't sure. She coached me on how to feel my stomach for the tightening and explained that once I felt the pain, the contraction, and the tightening of my stomach, to write down when it happened, every time it happened. She then said that when the contractions were 5 minutes apart, I needed to head to the emergency room right away and to call back. So that was it. I laid back in bed trying my best to rest and find a comfortable position, dozing off and on until my alarm woke me at 5 am.

While preparing to head to the hospital, the contractions were consistent. I got dressed and took one last look around the apartment, and told Adrian that when we come back, we will have our baby girl with us. We still had to drive to pick up my sister-in-law before heading to the hospital. She was a big part of my life and wanted to be there for the birth of my first child and I wanted and needed her there! She is such a strong person and had her first child with no drugs so I could also use the support. Even though it probably was not the best choice, I felt that only I could get there in record time quickly and safely, I didn't really trust Adrian's driving and to this day I still don't. As we got closer to the hospital, my contractions were barely 5 minutes apart. I moaned in pain while briefly closing my eyes and gripping the steering wheel. "Just pull over real quick and let me drive," Adrian said. "No!" I snapped. "I'm fine, we're almost there." He and my sister-in-law kept trying to convince me to pull over and let them take the wheel, but I was adamant, and kept driving. As I drove, I had one contraction after another, but we arrived at the hospital safely.

As I walked into the hospital to check in, reality started to settle in big time and so did the pressure. With every step, gravity seemed to grab hold of my lady parts. I was walking so slowly, the nurse asked if I wanted a wheelchair and surprisingly, I said no. I had read that it was good to walk as it gets closer to having the baby so I was determined to do what I could to help have an easy delivery. I also promised myself, Adrian, and my sister-in-law that I wouldn't get an epidural. Throughout my pregnancy I read so many negative and scary things about having an epidural and I wanted to have a full, natural pregnancy with no drugs, but all that went out the window once I dilated to 6 centimeters.

As the nurse prepped me to deliver my firstborn into the world, more fear set in. *Will I be okay, will my baby be okay, can I do this without drugs, and how bad is this really going to hurt?* As I got settled into the bed, I thought it was neat how I was able to see the intensity of the contractions as they started and diminished. Not that I needed to see it on a screen because I could feel the contractions as they became more intensified. Soon the doctor came in to see how I was doing and checked to see how much I dilated. The doctor was caring and gentle and I loved that. I felt very blessed to have her. I was 4 centimeters according to the doctor, and my water had not broken just yet.

I always had a vision in my head of my water breaking while I was driving in the car or in the store or something. Thank goodness I didn't have to live out one of those scenarios. When the doctor finally broke my water, it felt as if I had just peed all over myself, very warm and wet. Once my water broke, things got more intense. The contractions were stronger and more painful.

The next time the doctor came in to check me I had dilated to 6 centimeters. I was tossing and turning, grabbing hold of the bed, and Adrian's hand, and I can't remember how much I cursed but there were definitely curse words. My sister-in-law was so supportive and tried her best to help me not focus on the pain, but I had had enough and felt I couldn't take it anymore. My mom was also in the room and tried just as hard as Adrian and my sister-in-law to help me be strong and not get an epidural. I knew that I had to decide before I reached 8 centimeters, or I'd be out of luck and stuck with all the pain of contractions and pushing this baby out. "I want an epidural," I cried out. "Get the anesthesiologist!" I yelled. I got a lot of pushback from my support system in the room but ultimately it was my decision, and I felt the pain was insurmountable. "I want an epidural! I yelled even louder; I can't do this!"

I often wonder the outcome if I had been just a little stronger in that moment and had a little more faith and courage and yelled out what I could do instead of what I thought I couldn't. No matter how much support I had in the room, I felt I just could not go through with it because I wasn't strong enough and I didn't tolerate pain well at all. Never let someone make you feel as if you are weak or not as strong because your tolerance for pain is different than theirs. We all tolerate pain differently and, in that moment, the pain was too much for me to handle. Of course, the bible tells us that childbearing would be painful, but it also tells us that we can do all things through Christ that strengthens us. I should have repeated that scripture to myself over and over, but I was still strong and made the decision to get the relief I needed and by the grace of God, strong enough to continue birthing my child. I had also read about how an epidural can affect your body and how things can take a wrong turn.

Getting the epidural was one of the scariest experiences I've had in my life. Knowing a huge needle was being used and that there would be a tiny tube in my spine had me on edge big time. But I went through with it and thankfully it went just fine. I could actually just lay back and relax while watching the contraction monitor and say, "Wow, that was a big one," without even feeling how strong the contraction really was. It was such a strange feeling.

I couldn't really feel anything from the waist down, but I could still feel a bit of the pressure of the baby coming down further in the birth canal and I knew when I was ready to push. It was amazing. Once I told the nurse I thought the doctor should come to check me and that I felt like I needed to push, she took one look between my legs and said I was crowning, ran out to get the doctor and things moved like a whirlwind after that. The big bright light was turned on, they broke the bed down in front to prepare for the doctor to grab the baby, as nurses were running in and out bringing the things I would need after the delivery. It was bizarre to me to say the least. Adrian looked so nervous standing by the wall and out of the way of all the hustle and bustle and my sister-in-law was jumping up and down with excitement telling me how much hair the baby had because she could see the head starting to emerge. My poor mom was a ball of emotion. I could see the worry on her face as she was praying and asking God to be in the room. "LeTicia, it's almost time to push but I need you to wait until I tell you to" my doctor said. I felt the urge to push so bad, I also felt like I had just pooped myself and my sister confirmed that I did. This was so embarrassing. *YUCK!* I thought. The doctor said, "Don't worry about it, it's natural." I still felt disgusted and embarrassed regardless of how supportive everyone was being. *I need to make sure I have a good poop before the next baby so this won't happen again* I thought. "Push," the doctor said. I bared down and gave it all I had because it was kind of hard to feel how hard I was really pushing. The doctor instructed me to stop. *What, why?* I thought to myself. This pressure was not letting up and I was ready to push this baby out. "Okay, said the doctor, Push." I gave it two more pushes and my baby was here. I couldn't believe it. I pushed a total of three times and my baby girl was here, born at 10:59 am on June 19th. Ariah Monae Rivera-Clemente had made her way into this world, and as they laid her on my chest, all shiny and wet, I kissed her on her forehead and began sobbing, thanking God for my healthy, beautiful baby girl.

Ariah was the love I never knew. Sure, I loved her dad, and I've loved before, but not like this. I never wanted to put her down, and I could just stare at her little face and take in the smell of her forever. With God's help, she would be the one to truly show me how to listen, how to communicate, and how to be there for her and any other children I might have. She would be the one, the first, to take me down the beautiful path of motherhood and I could not be happier in that moment knowing she was mine and that God blessed me with the honor of being her mother.

"Children are a heritage from the Lord, offspring a reward from him."

Psalms 127:3 NIV

CHAPTER 3

The Wedding

July of 2006 came in the blink of an eye and after losing the baby the previous October, it was time to shift my focus to our wedding which was scheduled to take place on August 5, 2006. I was in full plan mode but on an extremely strict budget. Our reception was set to take place at a small community clubhouse where my grandmother lived, following a small ceremony that would only include our parents and grandparents. It was not what I had envisioned for myself or my future husband nor was it the wedding I had dreamt of having since I was a little girl.

Amid all the planning and finalizing, I began to feel weird sensations in my body. I was experiencing pains I had never felt in my stomach before. These weren't your typical period cramps, they were different. They were sporadic. One minute I'd be fine and the next I'd be in pain, not unbearable pain but enough pain to realize something wasn't' right. I also felt very fatigued. I didn't think anything of it because I thought it was a combination of stress and the start of my cycle, but my cycle never came. Initially when I realized I might be pregnant again I was excited, then the memories of my last pregnancy came roaring back. One day after work I decided to stop at a store and get a pregnancy test. Getting home to take the test and the what-ifs scenarios were all I could think about. *What if I'm pregnant again, will this baby be, ok? What if it's just stress?* My mind kept racing.

Finally, after picking up my daughter and making it home from work, I rushed to get in the door of our apartment, grabbed a snack for my daughter, and turned the television to one of her favorite shows. Once Ariah was settled, I went to the bathroom to take the pregnancy test. After peeing on the stick, I washed and dried my hands in what seemed like slow motion to keep myself from looking down at the pregnancy test too soon ...

Pregnant ... the test results showed pregnant. I didn't know what to do, think, or how to feel, so I did the only thing I could think to do at that moment, I prayed that everything would work out this time and waited for Adrian, my fiancé to get home to tell him the news.

After calling to schedule an appointment to confirm my positive test results, I went into the doctor a few days later, hoping they would do a sonogram (sono) immediately and tell me that the baby I was growing inside my womb was ok, but instead I was told that according to when I had my last cycle, I was around 5 weeks pregnant and that I would need to wait at least another week before they would be able to pick up anything on the sonogram. After another week went by, I went back to the doctor for the sonogram. I laid on the table and anxiously waited for the technician to pick up the baby's heartbeat after she smeared the warm gel on my belly. The silence was scary as I watched the screen for a glimpse of the tiny blur that may indicate a baby is there. She didn't say anything as she typed and moved the wand on my belly taking picture after picture. She then did a vaginal sonogram and told me that the doctor would discuss the sono with me.

Feeling anxious and afraid of what the doctor was going to say, I walked slowly down the hall to the room where I was told to wait for the doctor to come in. Finally, after waiting for what seemed like an hour, the doctor came into the room. "Hi, how are you today?" she asked. I told her I was fine and waited to hear what she had to say. "So, the sono didn't pick up a heartbeat and it didn't show us a baby just yet, it may still be too soon to tell," she said. She began to explain how she wanted me to return in 2 weeks and explained what signs to look out for should I be having a miscarriage or a tubal pregnancy. *A tubal pregnancy* I thought! It was as if I had entered the twilight zone because in my mind her voice became muffled as I tuned her out while only seeing her mouth move, and instead of listening to her I began listening to the voices in my head as they played out the worst-case scenarios. I didn't know what to say, I didn't have any questions, so I just told her thank you and she told me to take it easy and left the room. As I gathered my things and slipped my shoes on, I whispered a little prayer, "Lord, please let everything be ok with me and this baby."

Finally, wedding day was here! It was a little hard to focus with everything else I had going on and knowing I would have to return to the doctor the following week did not put my mind at ease. I wasn't nervous at all about the wedding, I was more disappointed than anything. I was in my feelings about not being able to have the wedding I really wanted and was concerned about my family and friends not being at the ceremony and worried about if they would have a good time at the reception. It was supposed to be my big day, our big day, and I just wanted all my friends and family to witness me marrying my best friend, the man that told me 5 years before that he always knew he was going to marry me.

Adrian and I had known each other since high school. We didn't attend the same high school but because we had mutual friends, we saw each other from time to time. Once we graduated, we lost touch until one night in April of 2001 when he saw me leaving 6th street walking back to my car. My kids love it when I tell the story of how we reconnected.

I feel that Adrian and I reconnecting was kismet because I almost didn't go out that night. Earlier that day I was hanging out at the Texas relays with some friends, and I had plans and was super excited to join the relay festivities later that night in downtown Austin with a different friend, but the plans changed. The person I was supposed to go downtown with said something else came up and that she wouldn't be able to go so I begged the friend I was hanging out with during the day to go with me that night, but she adamantly refused. I laugh to myself when I remember how much I tried to persuade her to go with me. I even ran into a movie theater later that night to find her while she was in the middle of watching and pleaded with her to go with me. She was not a fan of downtown Austin, let alone 6th street so the answer was still no.

Once it was determined that no one would be going out with me, I went back home where I lived with my grandmother at the time. Once inside I decided to shower and get comfortable, but I couldn't stop thinking about going downtown. I was literally looking at myself in the bathroom mirror pacing back and forth and thinking *I gotta go.* I guess I thought I would miss out on something and now looking back, I would have.

I finally decided I was going to go anyway. By the time I made up my mind it was after 11 pm. I knew there would be people down there that I would know and run into but I really didn't want to walk from my car to the clubs by myself so I called a good friend of mine, asked him if he would be down there and if he would meet me when I arrive so I don't have to walk alone and he said he would, so I was psyched again. Once I arrived, I called him from my cell, a pretty cool Nokia phone at the time. How times have changed. He met me at the lot where I'd parked and walked with me to where all the madness was, on the party goer filled street of 6th. He told me to let him know when I was ready to leave so he could walk me back to my car and we went our separate ways. While I was there, I popped into a few clubs, the ones I could get into at least, because I wasn't 21 just yet. After visiting with some people I knew, and running into a few old boyfriends, I said to myself "It's time to go." I was probably there for an hour, tops and thought *maybe I should have just stayed home.*

Once my friend met back up with me, he asked, "You're leaving already?" and I told him yes, that I should have just stayed home to begin with. As we were walking away from the crowded club lined street towards the parking lot under the bridge, I heard someone yell my name. I couldn't tell where it was coming from until I heard him yell my name again more loudly. It was Adrian! I saw him waving me over fanatically with a huge grin on his face. I guess he couldn't come over to me because he and his cousin were in a line to get into a club. Once I walked over, we hugged and looked at each other both surprised to see one another because it had been over a year since we last hung out or even spoke. I was fine as ever wearing a skintight black sleeveless blouse with a tight medium length multi-pattern skirt with a slight ruffle at the bottom that fell just above my knees. It was one of my favorite outfits that accentuated my curves in all the right ways. He had grown out his hair and was looking pretty good himself. After talking briefly and sharing each other's contact information he told me he was going to call me later and I walked away secretly excited. He did call, we talked and talked every night and on most nights until 2 am in the morning. He told me very early on, before we decided to date, that he knew he was going to marry me. He couldn't see the look on my face from the other side of the phone, but I thought he was crazy to think such a thing. But he was right.

As much as I tried to enjoy my wedding reception, I couldn't. I danced a little, I smiled a lot but all I kept thinking about was the strange aches and pains I was having on the left side of my stomach and how I had been feeling fatigued. It had me a little concerned, but I assumed it was just a normal part of pregnancy. My mind was filled with negative thoughts, not to mention negative comments that were made by family about the food, the fact that there was no alcohol, and how bored they were at the reception. I was ready to get the night over with. I wanted to go home, rest and look over the gifts we received and maybe even watch the video of the reception, but I still have not seen that video to this day.

If I thought ending the night and going home would be any better, I was wrong! As much as I wanted to, I couldn't have sex with my husband on the night of our wedding because I was instructed by the doctor to refrain from having sex until we knew more about what was going on with the pregnancy and with my body. After the wedding reception, a mutual friend of ours, a friend that we've known since we were kids who was more like a brother to Adrian, decided it would be a good idea to come hang out and spend the night with us and my husband obliged. They spent the night downstairs playing video games while I lay in bed left to worry about everything, alone.

This was not how I imagined my wedding night to play out. I had so many thoughts running through my head, and I wanted someone to share them with, someone who could understand what I was feeling and dealing with. It was difficult for me being in a space of uncertainty with my body and dealing with a potential ectopic pregnancy. The doctors seemed to not have the answers and I sure didn't have a clue what was happening at the time. All I could do was put my trust in God.

Do not be anxious about anything, but in every situation, by prayer and petition, with thanksgiving, present your requests to God. And the peace of God, which transcends all understanding, will guard your hearts and your minds in Christ Jesus.

Philippians 4:6-7 NIV

CHAPTER 4

Emergency

Shortly before the wedding Adrian and I moved into my father-in-law's home in South Austin to save some money and work on our credit so that we could purchase our first home. It was the summer of 2006, and our goal was to be in a new home sometime in 2007.

One night before going to bed I got in the shower and the strange pain I was having grew increasingly worse in what seemed like a matter of seconds. "Adrian!" I yelled out from the shower. I was holding on to the shower towel rack and the shower curtain, trying not to fall. I felt like I was going to pass out and there was pain shooting on the left side of my stomach. I could not stand up straight and I was crying from the immense pain I was feeling. Adrian ran in, grabbed a towel, and helped me get out of the shower and walked me to our room where he guided me to the bed to sit down. "I need to go to the emergency room," I told him, barely able to speak. All I could think about was the pain. He quickly assisted me with getting dressed then helped me walk to my daughter's room before we left. As I bent down in pain to kiss my daughter good night, I told her I loved her with tears in my eyes not knowing if that would be the last time I saw her. The pain was increasing so that I felt like I was going to die.

My father-in-law stayed with my daughter and Adrian rushed to get me into the car so that he could get me to the emergency room quickly. The drive to the hospital was a blur. I remember the worry in his voice as he told me repeatedly to hold on and stay with him while he sped through the streets of Austin to get me to the emergency room. I kept thinking *Lord, please don't let me die tonight.*

Once we arrived at the emergency room, I felt that I was drifting in and out of consciousness while Adrian ran in to get help. There were two nurses that came back to the car with him, and they somehow got me into a wheelchair and wheeled me into a curtained room. As I moaned and groaned from the pain I was experiencing, I was being asked questions by one of the nurses, but Adrian was able to answer most of the questions for me. One of the nurses was very rude and cold, so much so that I wondered how she could even be a nurse. She disregarded me and my pain and looked at me with irritation on her face as though she could not stand the fact that I was moaning in agony. She was very short with me, my mom and my husband when asking her questions about medication or when a doctor would come in, or how long until they come get me for the sonogram that was needed to see what was going on. She moved about the room in a swift agitated manner as if she did not want to be there. I didn't want to be there my damn self, but it was no way to be treated by a nurse and I will never forget how she made me feel. She made me feel like what was happening to me did not matter and like my pain was not important, like I was not important.

It felt like things were moving fast but at the

same time, not fast enough. I wanted to be rid of the pain I felt in that moment. The next thing I knew, I was being wheeled to another room with a sonographer. Unlike most rooms where sonograms are done, this room was cold, dark, and scary. The sonographer was calm and expressed how sorry she was that I was in pain. *You're much nicer than the nurse,* I thought to myself. She conducted an abdominal and vaginal sonogram which were both uncomfortable. The look of trepidation on her face as she moved the handheld probe around scared me. I knew that she knew what she was looking at while I on the other hand had no idea what was going on or what was about to happen. When I asked her what was happening to me, she said, "It may be an ectopic pregnancy, the doctor will explain more."

Back in the room where my husband was waiting for me, the doctor came in, I vaguely remember her saying to me that I needed to be taken into surgery immediately and explaining that I was having internal bleeding from the rupture that occurred from an ectopic pregnancy, which would explain why I was in so much pain. There was fear in my husband's eyes and all I could think in that moment was *God, please don't let anything happen to me* as they rushed me off to the operating room.

The next thing I remember happening was being in a hospital room and having a familiar face wake me. It was a doctor who was a partner with my OBGYN at the time. She had such a peaceful spirit about her, a comforting spirit that made me feel like everything was going to be ok, I was going to be ok. She took the time to explain that she was the doctor who performed my surgery and what she saw, and what she had to do. "I had to remove your left fallopian tube" she said. While showing me parts of bloody insides, she explained how the embryo was lodged in my fallopian tube where it started to grow which caused the rupture. She also told me it could happen again in the future on the other side and how basically any pregnancy from here on out would be high risk.

Of course, in that moment, all kinds of thoughts came rushing to my mind. Would I be able to conceive again? Would I have more miscarriages? And of course, the question I'm sure a lot of us ask, Why God is this happening to me? I would often blame myself and think, maybe I'm doing something wrong, or eating the wrong things. Am I not going to church enough or praying enough? The list goes on. After staying in the hospital for two days, I was released to go home. I was still in pain but this time it was from having laparoscopic surgery to remove the fallopian tube and now I would have to give my body time to heal. This meant no strenuous activities including sex, no heavy lifting, so I could not pick up my daughter and limiting gassy foods for a week or two. When we arrived back to my father -in- law's house it was a slow painful journey walking up the stairs. I took off work for two weeks to give myself time to heal and Adrian and my mom had to do a lot for me the next couple of days including bringing me food and taking Ariah to and from school.

At the time, Ariah was going to a Christian school where she was in pre-kindergarten classes. I absolutely loved it for her and most importantly

Ariah loved it there as well. Some days when picking her up she didn't want to leave. She had some amazing teachers that really loved her and all their students. They showed so much care and concern and prayed for and with the parents as well. During the two years she was enrolled I became close with one of the directors and was able to confide in her about my struggles with childbirth and spoke with her often about life in general. What I loved about her most was that she was great at listening without passing judgment and would often say things that would seem to lighten my load. Once I had gotten back to work and into the routine of dropping off and picking my daughter up again the director stopped to talk with me to let me know that she'd been praying for me and my situation and told me she had something that she would like to give me. It was a book. Little did I know this book would change my perspective and strengthen my faith regarding childbearing. The book was called "Supernatural Childbirth" by Jackie Mize. This book had very specific prayers and stories of healing. Prayers to heal, strengthen, and move mountains.

Some years down the line I later gave that book to a friend who also had struggles with childbearing so that it may be a blessing to her as it was for me.

Sometimes when things don't go how we expect or how we plan, some of us may tend to question God, without even thinking it could be happening for you and not to you and without considering there could be a bigger picture for what God has in store. "Supernatural Childbirth" really helped me get through some emotional turmoil, the recent loss, and encouraged me to stay faithful and put my trust in God. It helped me keep a positive perspective about the very first miscarriage I had and the recent tubal pregnancy. It would be the book that also helped me get through heartbreaking times ahead while helping me maintain a positive mind frame which can be difficult when you are struggling with something, and my struggles were conceiving and depression. Positive thinking didn't happen for me overnight, but I began to speak positive affirmations over my body, my womb, and my life while realizing God definitely had a master plan.

"'For I know the plans I have for you," declares the Lord, "plans to prosper you and not harm you, plans to give you hope and a future.'"

Jeremiah 29:11 NIV

CHAPTER 5

What Next?

July 10th, 2007 was a great day! My husband and I had just bought our first home together. I was 26 and Adrian was 25 and neither of us knew much then about the home buying process. When we were house hunting, we didn't really have a clue as to what we really wanted or what we should be asking. We did know that we had faith and that if it was meant to be, it would be. We had been working with a Realtor for a little over a month who had connected us with a great team that helped repair our credit while we were under contract for our new home.

The day we found our home, my husband felt it was the one almost immediately when he saw it. We toured a few other homes in the neighborhood and even in other communities but the house he was drawn to was a nice two-story on a corner lot that backed to a natural and protected green belt. Once inside the home, we looked around, stopped in every room to check out every feature, and looked around again. Once back downstairs in the living area, I asked our realtor if she could excuse us for a moment while we talked about it, so she stepped outside. At that very moment I said, "Lets pray" and we stood hand and hand and prayed, asking God that if it was meant for us, that He would move every obstacle and allow it to be so.

From that moment on I did not worry about a thing concerning our new home. I literally started packing before we even knew if we would be fully approved or not. It was so funny because people thought I was getting ahead of myself and some of my coworkers at the time were looking at me as if I had lost my mind as I gathered empty boxes to take home to use for packing. A few of my coworkers understood my faith and admired how I believed it would happen and how my faith was strong enough to pack with a purpose and without knowing if we would get our credit scores up enough since we were only conditionally approved. But it happened; we were approved and we moved into our four-bedroom home with our only child at the time, Ariah. God did not bless us with that big house for nothing. Having the faith I needed to believe my dream about owning a home was easy, yet I didn't seem to have the same measure of faith when it came to having another baby.

Even after my past two losses, I would still share my pregnancy troubles with my coworkers and many others. Just the thought of bringing another baby into the world excited me so much that I couldn't help sharing it with others. I think as my faith in having more children grew, it shined through the testimony of my loss as I told it to others.

It had been almost 2 ½ years since my last loss and still, no baby. My oldest was 6 and would be turning 7 in the summer of '09. In January of 2009, I suffered another miscarriage. I had a lot of people in my corner supporting me and my journey to have more children. I prayed my heart out when it came to asking God to bless me with another child, wondering when it would be my turn, if, it would be my turn. At times I watched other women and felt envious that they were doing the one thing I felt I was miserably failing at, that my body was failing at. It was hard. I was blessed in so many ways and had so much to be thankful for already yet, a piece of me felt annoyed, sad, and discontent with my current circumstances while simultaneously being happy for those around me who were having babies knowing that they could do the one thing that my body refused to do for me.

Over the years I had attended many women's retreats with my mom. It was a lot of fun and I enjoyed the support that all the women gave each other. We need more of this today. While attending the retreat, I would meet new people, hear different stories and testimonies, and enjoy good food. I'm always down to attend an event with great food. Over the years, my mom had shared my struggles with some of her fellow ladies in the ministry and one of them who happened to be attending the retreat at the time asked if they could pray with me. *I'll take all the prayer I can get* I thought to myself, as she reached for my hands. This lady that knew nothing about me, other than my issues with childbearing, prayed for me with true compassion and earnestness, I got chills and knew that God was there at that very moment, listening and speaking to my heart as we prayed. Have you ever had that feeling come over you where you know that you know that God is there with you!?

After she finished praying there were tears in my eyes. She asked me for my phone number so she could call and pray with me. My first thought was, *great, this lady is gonna be calling me every day now to pray,* in a sarcastic way. *Lord forgive me,* I thought to myself instantly. This lady prayed for me and had moved me to tears, of course I was going to give her my number. I told her yes and wrote down my number on a piece of paper and gave it to her. She called me from time to time and each time she did, I would literally go into my closet to receive the prayer and the word God wanted me to hear. Matthew 6:6 says "But when you pray, go into your room, close the door, and pray to your Father who is unseen. Then your Father, who sees what is done in secret, will reward you." So, after our calls, I would continue to pray in my closet, on the floor, on my knees, crying and even pleading with God at times to bless me with another child.

June 2009 had come, and I suffered another miscarriage. *What is wrong with me?* I thought. I was going over things in my mind that could help me rationalize why I was having such a hard time conceiving but not only conceiving, staying pregnant once I had conceived. I was in good health, I was not drinking, other than an occasional social drink, and I was still active and working out from time to time. So, I thought, *it's stress, it's got to be stress,* because my job at the time was definitely stressing me out. I was dealing with stressful working conditions and a horrible boss in a place that loomed like a dark cloud over my life.

Another dear friend of mine who was like an aunt or big sister to me would always call me and speak encouraging words as I was going through these difficult times. As I cried on the phone with her, she would remind me to be strong and keep the faith. She would say to me that He, (God) was going to give me another baby one day. She was always so confident when we spoke, as if God Himself told her it would be so. I wanted to believe her; I did believe her but there was still a little part of me that didn't. Part of me thought it would never happen but part of me believed He would hear my prayers and bless me with another child.

After having the miscarriage in June, I went to my OB to talk to her about my options for helping me to conceive, and she told me to start charting my ovulation by taking my temperature and scheduling sex with my husband. "*Schedule sex.* I thought, *that is not how it works with us,* but if that's what had to be done to get the child I so desired, then that's what we would do. The significance of taking my temperature was to find my basal body temperature which would indicate when I was ovulating hence indicating the best time to have sex hopefully increasing the chances of egg fertilization. I was encouraged to take my temperature in the mornings and keep graphs to show her my results. These graphs would help tell when I was ovulating and when would be the best time to conceive. For about two months I tried this method before Adrian and I made the decision to see a specialist, someone that could give us more insight into what was really going on with my body and if there was something more causing my miscarriages. After discussing this with my OB, she wrote me a referral to see an endocrinologist and suggested I show her the charting that I had been doing over the past couple of months as well.

In the beginning of September 2009, I made an appointment to go to the endocrinologist. An endocrinologist is a doctor that specializes in treating disorders of the endocrine system, such as hypothyroidism, diabetes, menopause, pituitary disorders, and much more. My hopes were that I'd be able to get some insight and more understanding of what was going on with my body. I couldn't help but think, *Yes! I'm finally going to get some answers on what the heck is going on with me.* Seeing that doctor was possibly the best thing I could have done, even though our visits were cut short by my lack of complete insurance coverage needed to continue and my inability to pay out of pocket. Going to a fertility specialist and receiving fertility treatment is expensive and I was not in a position financially to explore all my options.

I was only able to visit this specialist three or four times, but those appointments were very valuable. What I became aware of in that short amount of time was that for some reason my body had increased levels of prolactin. Just my first visit alone was enlightening. While conversing with the physician and speaking with her about my medical history, she explained things that were going on with my body in a way I could understand, and she showed me by squeezing my nipples that my breasts were secreting a clear fluid. She went on to explain how this was happening because of the increased levels of prolactin which causes your body to think you need to lactate. She also discovered that I carried the sickle cell trait, had possible ovarian dysfunction, I was positive for anti-cardiolipin antibodies which is basically a clotting issue, had Hx urticaria (another word for hives) and uterine fibroids. That was a mouth full, right? So, what in the world do all these things mean, and how is this keeping me from carrying another child? At the time it was a lot to think about and I had no idea what any of that stuff meant or how it was affecting my body.

For my second visit to the endocrinologist, I was asked that my husband accompany me so that he could do a series of blood tests as well as a semen test to make sure there wasn't anything going on medically on his end. Thankfully, Adrian did not carry the sickle cell trait and his little soldiers were just fine. One day after arriving to another appointment which I quickly found out would be my last appointment; while speaking to the attendant at the check-in window, I was told the insurance was no longer covering my appointments but that I could still continue seeing the specialist if I paid a certain amount of money. I left that check-in window that day in tears, feeling shut out and hopeless.

It was time for me to pick up my go-to book, "Supernatural Childbirth" for encouragement and faith strengthening, in addition to my bible. When I first began to read the book and read other stories of women who had similar challenges, I would think, *I hope I can tell my story and share my testimony one day and have more kids to tell it to.* As I read the book over and over while studying scriptures and praying, I went from hoping I can tell my story, to knowing I will be able to tell my story, and it was my faith that caused me to know I would, because I believed God for it, and I trusted that His Word is true.

Cast all your anxiety on him because he cares for you.

1 Peter 5:7 NIV

CHAPTER 6

Azriel

September 2009 had come and gone. It was a tough month for me since I had to stop seeing the endocrinologist, but I moved passed it and looked forward to God's promise over my womb. I was ready to start a new month because my birthday was right around the corner.

Adrian and I were on the road traveling from Austin to a small town outside of Corpus to take care of a ticket he had gotten a while back. Unfortunately, we had made that trip once a month, for the last 6 months and that day we were celebrating our last visit to pay off his deferred adjudication. On the way back to Austin, we stopped at one of my favorite Texas Mexican restaurants in San Antonio. It was one of my absolute favorite places to have a margarita, chips and salsa. I was excited to sit down to eat, I'm usually always excited to sit down and eat, but something didn't feel right when I ordered my margarita. Do you ever get a feeling, or hear "that" voice, when you are about to do something that you maybe shouldn't do? Kind of like when you were a kid, and your mom told you that you couldn't go outside to play but when she lays down to take a nap and you go to the door, something stops you and says "Don't you unlock that door and go outside" but you do it anyway? I really did this by the way. Well it was like that! I felt as if I shouldn't have had that drink and I know now that it was the Holy Spirit telling me not to have it because a few weeks later, I found out I was pregnant. I couldn't believe it; I was so excited. I was also frightened at the same time, but something in me said to stay faithful and fear not. I immediately contacted my physician and this time things were done differently, and better precautions were taken.

I was sent to a different clinic instead of the one I would have normally gone to in order to have my blood work taken so they could check my Human Chorionic Gonadotropin (HCG) levels. This is a hormone that is produced by the placenta after implantation that increases drastically in number with a healthy pregnancy. In the same year of 2009 after becoming pregnant in January which resulted in a miscarriage, then becoming pregnant again in June, while miscarrying, the physician checked my HCG levels at that time, and they were decreasing. When you have decreasing HCG levels, that indicates a pregnancy is there, but also explained how my body was getting rid of the pregnancy. I had a lot of blood work done and learned through my OB that the cause of this was due to my body not producing enough of the hormone called progesterone. Progesterone is a hormone that helps maintain the uterine lining throughout the pregnancy. Isn't it amazing? What's amazing to me is how our bodies just know what to do. Yes, it's science, but what a mighty and amazing God He is when I consider the intricacies of a woman's body and the ability to create another human life. That is amazing indeed.

After I went to have my blood drawn, waiting for a call back seemed like an eternity. I finally received a call later that afternoon about my HCG levels and they looked good. I was scheduled for an appointment to see the doctor and have a sonogram. My OB was definitely being more proactive this go round. I mean by this time, I had already had an ectopic pregnancy that resulted in the loss of my left fallopian tube, and three miscarriages, two within 5 months of each other, so it made me feel good to know my OB and her team of nurses were doing everything they could to help make this pregnancy a successful one.

Due to my previous history of miscarriages and the doctors now knowing I did not produce enough progesterone, they prescribed me pills to take called Prometrium. These pills would provide my body with the additional progesterone needed to strengthen the uterine wall during my first trimester and help ensure strong implantation of the egg to my uterine lining. Being that I was considered high risk and having to take Prometruim, my doctor wanted to see me more frequently than normal in the first trimester. This was certainly nerve-wracking but warranted. This also brought about negative self-talk/voices that brought doubt and worry but I knew I served a loving and giving God and that this felt like the pregnancy that would be different from the rest, one that would actually produce a healthy baby.

One night while still in my first trimester I awoke to mild cramping and the urge to pee. Anytime there was cramping I was afraid. My history with past pregnancies had created a fear that walked beside the same joyous emotion I had each time I was pregnant. I had a habit of looking at the tissue after wiping myself when using the bathroom to check to see if there was any blood or any weird discharge. That night, there was blood. "Lord God," I said, "please don't let this be a sign that something is wrong." I was terrified at that moment and my heart ached at the thought of losing another baby. I had to call the overnight nurse; no way was I going to wait until the next morning to speak to someone. When I finally got a nurse on the phone, I explained what I had seen after I wiped myself. I answered her questions and explained that it wasn't bright blood, or clotty and that it looked like discharge with streaks of blood in it. The nurse explained to me that this could very well be implantation spotting. "What"? I asked. She then went on to explain how it could be a good thing and that it may be spotting from the egg burrowing in the lining of my uterine wall. She told me that she had scheduled an appointment for me to come in to see the doctor the next day so they could investigate it further. I was so nervous the next day and could not wait for the doctor to see me and confirm what the nurse had told me the night before. My OB confirmed that implantation spotting is exactly what it was and according to her my HCG levels were looking great, doubling, and tripling just as they should. It was really happening. All I could say was, "Thank God" and I felt overjoyed.

After what felt like hundreds of doctor visits and sonograms later, I had finally made it! I was actually in my third trimester awaiting the arrival of our baby girl Azriel. Adrian and I found out we were having a girl and spent hours and days trying to decide what we would name her. We had agreed early on that we would name all our children with "A" names. We had written quite a few names down that we liked but one night while watching a popular reality show at the time, one of the kids' names on the show was Azriel. And no, we did not get it from Gargamel's cat on The Smurfs.

Things had been going great, until one day when I went in for another sonogram. This particular sonogram was the one where they checked out every inch of my growing baby. The sonographer measured her legs, arms, head, spine, you name it. She looked closer at the spine and the brain development but slowed down and started to take quite a few more pictures and measurements when looking at my baby's heart. So of course, I asked, "Is her heartbeat ok?" She explained that she was taking measurements of the heart and looking to make sure the correct number of arteries were there and that the doctor would go over everything with me in more detail. When my OB was out, I would see a different doctor on her team. They were both great and made me feel as if I had a team of doctors working for me who cared about my well-being and the health of my unborn baby. Once the doctor came in, he explained that there may be an issue with one of the ventricles of Azriel's heart, and in that moment, my own heart skipped a beat and I felt as if it had dropped to my stomach.

He said that he wanted me to go see a specialist to examine the baby's heart while in the womb, just to be sure her heart was developing normally. Once I saw the specialist, he did confirm that there was something going on with Azriel's heart but said that I shouldn't worry and they would keep a close eye on everything, as that was all that could be done at the moment. He also explained that once she arrived, they would have to place a heart monitor on her for a few days to monitor her heart to help them find any problems or irregularities.

My pregnancy with Azriel had gone pretty normal, despite the numerous appointments and sonograms. Other than the discovered heart concern, I was in good health and so was she and I could not wait for her arrival. My due date was July 25th, which I thought was cool because that is also my mom's birthday, but I had a feeling she would come sooner. As time got closer to the due date I started to prepare. I made sure I had a hospital bag ready with clothes for myself and the baby and that bag was already in the car. I also made sure Ariah had some extra clothes in case she and Adrian spent the night at the hospital. On the morning of July 16th, something told me to prepare.

That afternoon, I started to braid Ariah's hair because I wanted to make sure it didn't need to be done while I was in the hospital and in the few weeks to come. This would save me time and be a nice convenience for myself and my husband. While braiding Ariah's hair around 1 pm, I started to feel contractions. Although it had been a while since I'd felt them, that's a feeling that is very familiar once it hits you and you just never forget what they feel like, at least I didn't anyway. I moaned in pain and my daughter Ariah turned around and looked at me and asked if I was ok. I smiled and nodded and just tried to ignore the pain until the next one came around about 17 minutes later. At that point, I was uncomfortable, and I knew that would be the day. I hurriedly continued braiding my daughter's hair and once finished, told her I was going to call her dad and that I was going to take a quick shower. I told my daughter to put on some shoes and to be ready because we were going to be going to the hospital.

The contractions were getting closer and were about 11 minutes apart when I had gotten out of the shower around 4 pm. I called my husband to find out when he thought his workday may end and told him we needed to go to the hospital as soon as he got home from work. I also told him that I had called the nurse and they were expecting me to arrive around 6 pm that evening. As we were pulling up to the hospital, my nervousness and anxiety kicked in and my contractions were five minutes apart. Once in the room and after changing into that oh-so-lovely hospital gown, the nurse was moving quickly to get the monitors on my stomach. Soon the doctor came in to check me and told me I was five centimeters dilated. I could not believe it, *this is actually happening*, I thought, *I'm having another baby*.

While thanking God and trying not to panic in that moment, I felt the contractions getting stronger and the nurses were telling me to hang in there and that they would be back to check me soon. Finally, around 8 pm, the doctor comes back in to check me again and tells me I was dilated to 6 centimeters. I immediately told her that I cannot take it anymore and that I definitely wanted an epidural. I am not a fan of any kind of pain, even though I tried to tell myself I could do it, but I just couldn't handle the intense, persistent, cramping. It literally felt as if gravity had grabbed hold of everything down there and was trying to pull out my uterus, I can't describe it any other way.

After waiting a few hours, the doctors gave me Pitocin which is a synthetic version of the hormone oxytocin that aids in stimulating contractions. The doctor also had to manually break my water. They had to do this for my first birth with Ariah as well. What a weird feeling that was. It made me feel a little crampy and I instantly felt like I had peed the bed. The contractions came harder and stronger with

more intensity once my water had been broken.
Where is that anesthesiologist? I thought to myself.
The time had finally come to get some relief. Once I
had the epidural, I expected things to slow down a
bit but a little after 9 pm the doctor checked me
again and said it won't be long, as I had gotten to 8
centimeters. *This was moving right along,* I thought.
Thank God.

A little after 10 pm I told the nurse that I was
feeling pressure and thought I needed to push. She
called in the doctor to check me, and it was go time!
The bright lights came on, nurses rushed in like a
whirlwind, and they prepared the bed for delivery
and my doctor got in position. It was a bit scary
seeing everyone move around so quickly but this was
the moment I'd been waiting and praying for, and I
felt God's presence and knew He was in control.
The doctor instructed me to push as my husband,
mom, sister-in-law and 8-year-old daughter watched
anxiously in the background. I pushed for a while,
and I could see the doctor and nurses were looking a
bit concerned. The doctor said to me, "Sweetie, I

think we may need to do a c-section." "Oh no we're not," I said. She explained some of the things that could go wrong if I continued to push, like hemorrhaging, stress on the baby and so on and at that moment I asked her to let me talk to my family. The doctor said she would step out for a minute but that we needed to decide quickly and that she would be right back.

At that very moment everyone gathered around my bedside, held hands, and prayed. My mother led the prayer and I felt in my heart and knew for a fact I was not going to get a c-section. When you know, you know. The doctor came back into the room and said okay, let's give it a few more pushes. She confirmed that baby was still okay and told me If I wanted to push, that I could try a few more times. As the doctor positioned herself at the end of my bed, I felt that strong, undeniable urge to push. I knew this was going to happen for sure. "Bare down and push" the doctor repeated a few times. "Wait, wait, I need you to stop pushing" she said. *What do you mean wait?* I thought to myself. The doctor said the head was out and after a few more pushes, I felt a huge relief of pressure followed by suctioning and a loud cry. She was here, Azriel was finally here!

After the doctor finished up, she walked to my bedside to congratulate me and said, "That was some amazing prayer you guys prayed". I smiled and said, "Yes it was, prayer works." We shared a smile. The nurses were still buzzing around the room and the doctor proceeded to check me to make sure I had delivered the placenta. Things got a little scary again because she and the nurses started to whisper and the look on her face showed concern. "LeTicia," my doctor said solemnly, "We are having some trouble getting the placenta out, but I don't want you to worry, I want you to breathe and relax." *Now how do you expect me to do that after telling me that?* I thought to myself.

Nurses were still buzzing around, running in and out of the room and everyone including my family had a look of fret on their faces. I was not at all ready for nor expecting what happened next. The doctor literally reached her entire arm up to the elbow into my vagina up my cervix to feel for the placenta and assist with its release. Even though I had the epidural I could feel pressure, and an uncomfortable sweeping motion of the doctor moving her hand inside my uterus doing her best to carefully remove the placenta from my uterine wall. I was horrified thinking about all the things that could happen and how I could bleed to death if something goes wrong. But by the grace of God, she removed it, and I felt a large blob of warmth being released.

I was so happy and relieved that Azriel was here, and that the scary part was over. I could just stare at her for hours and couldn't wait to get her home. When it was time to take Azriel in to see the pediatrician, she mentioned how she heard a murmur in her heart, and we discussed what had been discovered while I was pregnant with her regarding the possibility of a ventricle defect. She asked if I noticed anything alarming while she was sleeping or eating. I told her no, and that she seemed to be doing very well and that she was feeding well. The doctor informed Adrian and I that she was going to refer her to a baby heart specialist to have a scan done of her heart and told us they would more than likely want to place a heart monitor on her to get a better read of what it is her heart was doing. Once we saw the heart specialist, we were told Azriel would have to wear a tiny monitor with small electrode patches placed on certain places on her delicate baby skin. I hated seeing this, but I knew it was only temporary, but this scared me. I cried one day as I sat on the couch after changing her clothes and seeing the wires and her little body lying there on my legs incapable of knowing what was going on. "I know God did not bless me with her only to take her from me" I cried as my mother tried to console me. For a few months we continued to visit the heart specialist so they could keep an eye on Azriel's heart as she grew and finally our appointments began to spread out to where we only needed to do follow-up visits once a year. Adrian and I were relieved. The doctor mentions her murmur from time to time but thankfully she continued to grow as she should, strong, and healthy. Later that night, my father-in-law came to see Azriel and bring me food. Him bringing me food was one of the best parts of pregnancy and birthing his grandchildren.

I prayed for this child, and the Lord has granted me

what I asked of him.

1 Samuel 1:27 NIV

CHAPTER 7

Methotrexate?

I was overjoyed. The child I had been praying for all these years was finally here. It was amazing. Here was this tiny blessing that I couldn't help but stare at while holding her, covering her sweet little face with kisses. I've always heard people say, "Don't kiss the baby on the face", but there was no way that was not going to happen. I was going to shower my baby with kisses. My six months of maternity leave had flown by like a shooting star that you barely catch a glimpse of. I mean it really felt that fast. I cried so much knowing I'd be returning to the dungeon, only to be overworked and disrespected all while trying to think happy thoughts of returning to my baby at the end of the day.

While I worked, Azriel stayed with my grandmother which was a tremendous blessing. To have one of the most cherished women in my life watch after my daughter meant the world to me, but this was short-lived. After arriving to pick up Azriel from my grandmother one day after work, she explained to me that she would have to return back to work soon. My heart literally dropped to my stomach! *What was I going to do?* I thought. There was no way I was going to leave my three-month-old baby with anyone else and I certainly wasn't about to put her in some daycare. *This was more stress than I could handle,* I thought.

I was crying nearly every day and sometimes uncontrollably. I didn't want to go to work because I was miserable there, and I had to figure out who was going to keep my precious baby once my grandmother returned to work, all while trying to juggle taking care of my household, husband and two kids. I felt hopeless and tired and the thought of ending my life so that I wouldn't have to deal with all this stress too often crept into my mind. *What is wrong with me?* I thought, *what am I saying right now?* I literally played different scenarios in my mind of how and when I could do it. Maybe I'll get in the tub and slit my wrist, maybe I could just take a bunch of pills and have a glass of wine before bed. Thoughts of throwing myself out of a window or off a bridge. I even thought of driving off of a few bridges while driving alone from time to time. *Is this postpartum depression?* I thought. "What is wrong with me?" I asked myself while sitting on the side of my bed, crying into my hands. My husband was worried and suggested I talk to my doctor. "No way" I told him, I'll be fine." I told him this over and over again. I didn't want to talk to anyone about it, especially not a doctor. I was in such a panic that I would feel my heart starting to race. As I sat on the edge of the bed, I had strong intense pains in my back. What felt like kidney palpitations and prickly needle feelings under my armpits. *What is happening to me? Is this anxiety?* I thought.

I was afraid of what someone might think or that the doctor would admit me or have me committed and that I'd be taken away from my babies or worse, prescribe me some kind of drug that would put me in a zombie state of mind. I didn't see any of that for myself. I wasn't having any of that. So, I ignored my thoughts and the signals my body was sending me and carried on as if nothing was wrong.

It was December of 2010 and Azriel was about 5 months now and I was still hanging in there breastfeeding. With my first daughter, Ariah, I breastfed until she was six months old, and I was determined to do the same, if not more, for the rest of my children. Azriel had a healthy appetite that kept me feeding her every two hours, sometimes every thirty to forty-five minutes. I pumped every 3 hours at work until pumping at work became a challenge. I started noticing I wasn't getting the same number of ounces while pumping, then Azriel began to feed for longer periods of time. To me, this indicated my milk supply was low. I began to increase my water intake thinking this would help because I knew I wasn't drinking enough. *I hope this works*, I thought. I even took a picture of Azriel into work with me in my bag, along with one of her onesies to have in the room while I pumped. I thought this would alert my senses and encourage my milk to flow abundantly. It was great that I actually had a place to pump at work, however it was challenging to pump in the space provided. It was a cold shared space behind a door that used to be the janitor's closet. Their idea of providing privacy was to hang some thin, old and ugly curtain that had been through some things to divide one mother's area from the next. You could literally hear every single thing each person was doing while pumping and preparing milk. To top it off, it was a room within a larger room so there was no ceiling which meant it was not completely closed off. You could hear other people as they entered the lounge and restroom areas. As if that weren't bad enough, the chairs in the room were very uncomfortable. They were old antique school desks with an immovable top or seat that I had to slide in and out of. The space was so pitiful and only two women could pump at a time.

After about a week of not pumping enough milk, I thought it was time to go to the doctor to see if there was something going on. The doctor asked me some questions and decided to run a few tests, one of them being a pregnancy test. *No way could I be pregnant,* I thought. The doctor let me know that the nurse would call me to let me know if there was anything to be concerned about. She also advised me that I could start taking a pill to help increase my milk production, but I decided against it. I'm not one to jump at taking pills for a quick fix of anything, I'll suffer with a headache and any other kind of pain if I can bear it, so I chose to wait to see what the nurse said when she called with the results and doctor recommendation. Once the nurse called, I was nervous about what she would say. She told me that I was pregnant! "What?!" I said, "Yep," she said with laughter. "Wow!" "I just wasn't expecting that at all," I told her. She went on to tell me that the doctor had instructed me to go in to have more blood work done first thing in the morning to check my levels. *Of course,* I thought, and I was thankful to have a doctor that was proactive and actually showed concern because sadly, some doctors did not.

Once the blood test had been done, the nurse called again to confirm my pregnancy but said the

HCG numbers were not where they should be and that the doctor wanted me to come in to have a sonogram done. *Not again*, I thought. I scheduled my next appointment with the nurse and waited on pins and needles till the day of my appointment and sonogram.

When I went in to see the doctor, they were unable to see or pick up a heartbeat, they tried to see if they saw a sac in my uterus and it appeared there was a small sac, but it was just too soon to tell, the doctor said. The doctor instructed me to go have blood work again in two days to check on my HCG levels again to see if they were increasing as they should be, and when I did, the numbers went up but not significantly which was cause for concern. At my next appointment, the doctor explained she felt that I may be having another tubal pregnancy. My heart sank and I think she saw it on my face because she immediately ensued saying, "But I think we've caught it in time." I absolutely loved that physician; she was by far the most caring and gentle spirited doctor I've ever had. My husband would always tell me how I seemed to get the best doctors and he got the short end of the stick when it came to finding a good doctor in general. It was just something about her nature, you could just feel how she loved what she did, and it showed through her work and her words.

The doctor went on to explain how she thought the best thing would be for her to go in and remove the blockage, a fertilized egg, from my fallopian tube and said that she would place me on the schedule to have the procedure done. I wasn't sure what to think or how to feel at that moment, all I could do was just pray that all would go as the Lord planned and that I would live through the procedure and be able to try for another baby.

The day came for me to report to the hospital for the surgery and my husband was there by my side. They explained that it was an outpatient procedure and that I'd spend some time in recovery before being released to go home. The nurse took me to my room where I undressed and got prepped for surgery. I put on that familiar hospital gown and hair cap along with those too loose socks with the grips on the bottom and the top and lay there talking to my husband while waiting for the doctor to come in and speak with us before taking me to surgery. I was wondering when they were going to come and run the IV; I always got anxious thinking about that IV going in my arm.

When the doctor came in, she greeted my husband and I with a look of uncertainty. This made me a little uneasy but as she began to speak with that soft and kind voice, I began to feel better. "I don't think we should go through with the procedure," she said. "What?" I asked. The doctor explained that doing the procedure was risky because if she were to go in and the blockage was worse than she thought, the chance of her having to remove my entire tube was very likely. She went on to say that she thought there was another option that might work better for me and would save my tube and basically clean it out in a sense. The doctor went on to explain that I would receive a large shot in my hip called methotrexate. She explained that methotrexate is a drug used for different types of cancers, but it has other uses as well. She went on to say how she believed the drug would clear the tissue and the fertilized egg, from my fallopian tube. To be sure the drug is working I would have to go have my blood drawn for a few days to be sure my HCG levels were decreasing, which essentially means the fertilized egg is no longer growing thus decreasing the chance of the ectopic pregnancy and the egg would eventually dissipate.

This was a lot to take in, but I trusted her and truly felt that God placed an amazing doctor in my life at the right time. After putting my clothes back on, we were told to go to the doctor's office on the other side of the hospital so that her nurse could administer the shot. I was so nervous; I hate needles and all I could think of was the pain I was going to feel. *Just think about having a positive outcome,* I thought, but that was so very hard for me to do.

The nurse came in with a tray that had a huge vial of liquid, methotrexate, along with a very large needle. She explained what the medicine was and how they thought it would help, just as the doctor did, and then she went on to explain where the shot would be administered and that it was going to hurt. *Oh, I already know* I thought, but it was nice of her to tell me straight up what to expect. To her, I said, "Of course it's going to hurt, look at the size of that needle." She giggled a little and said, "I'm sorry, but just think of the end result." *Easier said than done* I thought. She told me to lay over the side of the table and to pull my pants down slightly exposing my buttocks. I thought to myself, *why did the shot have to go there, I mean really?* Something about it being the best place because of your large butt muscle? I didn't know. I guess I should have asked that question. "Take a deep breath and relax" she said, right before stabbing me in my butt with a ten-inch needle. Okay, I'm exaggerating, but it felt like I was being stabbed with a ten-inch needle. Oh my gosh it hurt so bad that I literally started to cry. Not like a sobbing, whimpering cry, but tears. Yes, tears were flowing from my eyes. "*Lord, have mercy*" I thought. I am such a wimp when it comes to pain, I really don't even know how I dealt with childbirth. Okay well, maybe the epidural had a little to do with it.

"I'm sorry, the nurse said with a saddened look on her face. I know it's pretty painful."

"That's an understatement" I said to her.

She laughed a little. The nurse explained that I may have some nausea, diarrhea, stomach upset, and tiredness and I experienced all of it. *I'm so glad I don't have to go to work tomorrow* I thought.

A few days had passed, and I went to the doctor to have my blood drawn as I was told. It worked, it actually worked! The shot of methotrexate had done what I was told it would do. I was overjoyed and ecstatic that I didn't have to go through another surgery. When I found out just three short months later I was pregnant again, I knew for sure the medicine worked and did what it was supposed to do.

Nevertheless, I will bring health and healing to it; I will heal my people and will let them enjoy abundant peace and security.

Jeremiah 33:6 NIV

CHAPTER 8

Aaliyah

There I was, lying in the doctor's office, waiting for confirmation of what I already knew to be true. I am pregnant again! I was literally dancing with excitement on the inside. I even did a quick little jig there in the mirror before the doctor came in while thanking God and laughing to myself, at myself.

"Congratulations" said the doctor, as she walked in the room with a loving smile on her face. I was so happy to have her as my doctor for this pregnancy since she had just helped me through the last ordeal with my 2nd tubal pregnancy. She was also the same doctor that conducted the emergency surgery when I had my first ectopic pregnancy that nearly killed me. She knew my history and genuinely cared about me and my health and the health of my unborn child.

By this time, it was April of 2011. I had quit my

job, pulled out all my retirement funds and made a vow never to return to that particular sector of state government again, and I never did. I didn't know exactly what I was going to do but I knew we had money to last a while even though I'd be penalized heavily with taxes for pulling my money early. What was most important was my mental and physical health and I had faith that this pregnancy would go well, and we would get over whatever financial hurdles that came our way during my time of unemployment.

The pregnancy with Aaliyah, soon to be my third girl, went smoothly. I didn't have any complications, and she was growing as she should. Believe it or not I only gained nineteen pounds throughout my entire pregnancy. Thankfully, morning sickness only lasted through my 1st trimester, and for the most part I felt great and full of energy. I believe one of the reasons I had such a great pregnancy is because I didn't have the stress of going to a job I hated every day. The pregnancy was so great that it seemed to pass very quickly and before I knew it, I was nine months, two centimeters dilated for 2 weeks, and having days of false labor until finally one night I felt that familiar pain and gravity pull below.

Adrian and I were lying in bed on a Tuesday night in January, and I kept feeling my stomach tighten while telling him to feel how rock-hard it was. I told him that I didn't think this was another false alarm and that we should head to the hospital. We grabbed our two girls and an overnight bag, hopped in the SUV and headed to the Emergency Room. I called ahead and was advised by the nurse to enter through the ER doors.

Once at the hospital they got me to a room pretty quickly and the contractions were pretty steady. The nurses got me settled into a hospital gown and placed a monitor on my stomach and let me know the doctor would come in to check on me shortly. I was so relieved that my same sweet, caring OB that I had been seeing was the doctor on call that night and that she would be the one to deliver my sweet Aaliyah. How blessed was I?

Over 5 hours and an epidural later, the time had finally come for me to push, I remember feeling more pain than I felt with the last two births, I mean, didn't I have an epidural? *Why am I hurting more than I remember,* I thought to myself. The doctor instructed me to push, and push some more. My daughter was coming into this world, and I could feel the pressure and burn of my flesh stretching and tearing. *This is definitely not what I expected* I thought. That epidural was surely wearing off but thank God, I couldn't feel it all.

Aaliyah came into this world at 5:14 am quietly, not making a sound, with those wide eyes as if she was wondering where she was and what was going on. She had a peace about her that was calming and didn't want to eat much just yet. The nurses had to keep her longer than I liked because her body temperature was lower than normal for an infant, so they said they needed to keep her in a warmer. While she was in the room with me, I had to keep her wrapped snug and hold her close to me. At times we did skin-to-skin contact to see if it would help her want to eat more or warm her up but to no avail, and for some reason her temperature would not hold at a safe range.

Finally, a few days later, it was time to get out of this hospital and go home. I must say, I did like the food, but I just wanted to get to my own bed and be in the comfort of my own home. The doctors were still concerned about Aaliyah's temperature. It had gotten to where it needed to be in order for us to be released, but the doctor instructed me to take Aaliyah to a pediatrician the very next morning to be seen.

When we brought her home, I watched her very closely. I was concerned because she didn't really latch or feed well in the beginning, and she seemed to be almost lethargic. While lying in her crib, she never cried that day, her eyes seemed to wander, and she just didn't seem all there to me. I held her for what seemed like most of the day. I prayed, I talked to her, I talked to God, and I asked for answers. I couldn't sleep at all that night and kept watch over her while she lay in the bassinet next to our bed.

The next morning, my husband and I arrived at the pediatrician's office with Aaliyah and the doctor was very concerned. Her temperature had dropped again, and she had lost a few ounces. "You need to take your baby back to the hospital; she will need to be admitted to Neonatal Intensive Care Unit (NICU)." My heart dropped, and I began to cry and asked if she was going to be okay. The doctor told me that he couldn't give me an explanation as to what may be going on with her but that she will be fine in the NICU and hopefully they would have more answers for me about her condition.

When we arrived at the hospital to take Aaliyah to the NICU, the nurses were all very nice and caring, showing lots of thought and concern for our situation and in a way that was comforting and reassuring. They explained everything they were doing as they were doing it, as well as the test they'd be running to try to get more answers as to why her body temperature kept dropping and why she was so lethargic. I couldn't stand to see her lying there helpless, then I looked around to some of the other babies, some who were fighting for their lives and the parents who stood watching nervously in sadness. I tried my best to be positive at that moment and told myself that it could be much worse, but that didn't help. I didn't want my baby to be in there at all. *Hadn't I gone through enough to have her?* I couldn't help but ask this question and I tried my best not to question God or ask why me, but in that moment, when I didn't know what was wrong with my baby or what the outcome would be, I questioned everything.

The hospital allowed me to stay in the postpartum wing so that I could be there every day, rest, and walk down to attempt to feed Aaliyah and like clockwork, I was there every 2 or 4 hours to feed her my pre-pumped breastmilk with an amazing pump provided by the hospital. I was pretty adamant about not leaving my baby and was grateful they allowed me to stay there. Aaliyah was too weak to latch properly and didn't really show any interest in wanting to breastfeed. This made me so sad because I knew my milk was the best for her but with me not being able to produce enough milk we had to supplement and that was heartbreaking. I knew she needed all the nutrients she could get, so I had no choice but to get her to drink the formula for now.

Day one of being in the hospital was hard, with all the uncertainty, worry and emotions and not knowing what exactly was wrong with our baby girl. While I stayed at the hospital, my husband Adrian took care of the other girls with the help and support of our families. This was a lot for him, me not being home with our newborn and him having to come back and forth to the hospital. One night when they came to see us in the hospital, my husband, Ariah and Azriel spent the night in my room. Azriel was 18 months old at the time. She began potty training before Aaliyah had arrived and was doing really well wearing panties during the day and pull-ups at night but the one thing she wasn't quite ready for was to be stripped of her beloved pacifier. This was her comfort, her peace and her dad decided to take it away during a time I felt she may have needed it most. *Why now* I thought? I think he just needed something to control with everything else going on being out of his control. This time was difficult for everyone close to us.

Day two of Aaliyah being in the NICU was not much different from day one. The doctors had drawn blood and run tests and still couldn't provide me with concrete answers as to what was going on with my baby girl. A doctor said that it may be some sort of virus. It was so frustrating not knowing exactly what it was but miraculously, her color started to come back, her temperature was steady, and she started to liven up a little and eat more which were all very good signs. God was in control and in times like these when no one has all the answers all you can do is have faith and trust that God does! The doctors told us they wanted to monitor her for another day and that if there was no change, we could go home the next day. I was so happy to hear the word home, all I could think about was getting into my own bed and placing my sweet baby girl in hers.

Day three, I was signing the discharge papers and could not wait to take Aaliyah out of there and go home with my family. During the last three days, I was also monitored very closely and was having issues with my blood pressure. Just the day before, my OB came to see me in the hospital room to check on us and to see if my blood pressure was still elevated. Fortunately, I was able to go home but was told to monitor my pressure myself and if I felt it was getting worse to come back and see her. When we finally got home with Aaliyah, I remember telling my husband while walking through the door that something wasn't right and that I had a pounding headache. I knew that it had to be my blood pressure, so I made the call. My blood pressure remained high and it was so strange to me because during the pregnancy it was fine. I told my husband we needed to go to the doctor. We were literally home for less than an hour. Once at the doctor, one of the OBs I'd seen regularly checked my blood pressure three times, and I could tell by the silence something was wrong. "I'm so sorry to tell you this and I know this isn't what you want to hear but your blood pressure is dangerously high, and I have to admit you to the hospital right away."

"What?" I asked.

I immediately began to cry in disbelief while staring at my kids, just wanting to be home with them and to do nothing else.

The OB explained that I ran the risk of having a seizure and needed to be treated with magnesium sulfate intravenously to prevent that. I was scared and frustrated all at the same time. The OB then went on to explain the risks of not being treated as well as some of the risks of the medication. I was mostly disappointed that I could not breastfeed my newborn baby who had just gotten discharged from NICU. The OB told me that I would be able to pump but only after a certain amount of time had passed and I had pumped and dumped the first round to keep her from getting exposed to any of the medication entering my body, so we had to supplement yet again.

As trying as this time was for me, I thanked God that I was alive and prayed and begged him not to take me away from my kids. There was a moment when I was laying there being pumped with meds when I literally thought it was the end for me and because I could hardly move and felt like there was a heavy weighted blanket on my head and my brain was foggy, I felt that I was going to die. I was torpid, and slowly whispering to Ariah, my oldest daughter who was nine at the time, "Should anything happen to me, please help dad with the babies and lead by example as a big sister." She had so much sadness in her eyes and kept repeating, "no mom." As she put her head on my chest, I closed my eyes and drifted off to sleep.

Waking up in darkness with only the light peering in from the hall and from the lights of the machines, I had no idea what time it was. It felt like it had been the slowest, most dreadful night and I didn't know what to expect next. My OB had come to check in on me and said the worst part was over. After being kept in the hospital for three days, I was finally able to return home. Maybe now I could have some normality with my family and have some peace, but sickness had not left me just yet.

One afternoon in March, not even three months after having Aaliyah, I had gone down to the courthouse to take care of a ticket I had gotten when I was pregnant with her. While standing in line holding the hand of my 20-month-old and barely hanging on to the car seat of my newborn in the other, I felt faint and nauseous. After speaking with a clerk and taking care of my ticket. I wanted to run outta there and jump in my car. I felt so bad and barely had the energy to hold the car seat let alone take a step forward. I remember saying over and over to myself in my head, *you've gotta make it, you've gotta make it, you're almost there, you're almost there.* The way I was feeling, that walk from the door of the courthouse to my car in the parking lot felt more like a 2-mile walk in 90-degree heat.

As I got closer to my car, I felt my grip slipping on the car seat. I became faint and extremely nauseous to where my mouth was watering. I made it to my car just in time to open the door and gently tossed both kids in the back seat just before I barreled over in pain and vomited on the pavement.

I made a call to my husband who to my surprise was already in route to the courthouse to help me with the kids. I explained to him how I was feeling and told him something was very wrong and that he needed to call 911. The ambulance showed up quickly and thankfully my husband wasn't far behind them. The paramedics began to assess my ailments and asked a series of questions as they began to place me on the gurney and prepare an IV. I explained how much my stomach was hurting and that I had thrown up and felt that it was going to happen again. They gave me something for my nausea and to help with the vomiting and I asked them if I was going to be okay, as if they knew. The paramedic tried to assure me that I would be fine and that they would take good care of me, but I didn't really believe it because of the pain and feeling sick to my stomach; I had no idea what was wrong with me.

The ride to the hospital was short and whatever they gave me for pain had me in a calmed state and I was no longer hurting. Once we arrived, they rolled me in quickly and explained to the nurse what was going on. They rolled me into a private room where they asked me more questions, hooked me up to all sorts of machines and placed different bags on the hook to go into my IV. I was eventually taken to a different room where a sonographer performed a sonogram to see what was going on in my stomach, she didn't say much, and she didn't have to because her face said it all. I knew what I saw on the screen wasn't normal. I asked the nurse what she was looking at and she explained she was looking at my gallbladder which appeared to have many stones. Many was an understatement, there were at least 20 or more. The nurse explained that she couldn't go into any detail, but it looked like I'd had them for a while and that the doctor would be able to give me more information. She asked me if my OBGYN ever saw anything while looking at my sonograms with my recent baby and I told her no. *How could they have missed that,* I thought. *I'm no doctor and even I could see what I was looking at wasn't normal.*

After taking me back to the emergency area, I was greeted by a doctor who told me I had to be admitted and have emergency surgery right away. *I can't believe this*, I thought to myself. *I just want to be at home with my kids and my newborn and now I have to be admitted to the hospital and stay in here for God knows how long.* I felt so defeated and the look on my husband's face matched how I was feeling.

So many thoughts went through my mind as I was being rolled to emergency surgery. *How can I still have so much faith and trust in God but still worry about coming out alive? Will my life be cut short by gallstones? Will I leave my kids with no mother to raise them or share in life's moments? Will my body function as it should after this surgery? Will I have to change my eating habits, and will I still be able to eat pizza?* Funny, not funny, but those are actually some of the thoughts I had prior to counting backwards from 100, which I only remember making it to 98.

Once I was out of surgery and back in my room, I was relieved to be surrounded by my babies, my husband, and my mother and stepdad. They all

looked worried and relieved at the same time. The
nurses had brought in a breast pump so that I could
pump and dump meds and to help keep my milk
production up, and pump to store milk for Aaliyah.
The nurse also brought to my attention that I now
had a drain in the right side of my stomach that was
put there to help the surgery incision drain fluid
from the area. It was so gross looking, and I was
terrified that I would accidentally yank it out or cause
more harm to myself.

It was so hard to think positive in those
moments because I couldn't care for my baby the
way that I wanted to, on my terms and in my own
home and it only made my depression worse. The
sadness that loomed over my head like a heavy rain
cloud was real and I felt that no matter what happy
thoughts I tried to drum up or how often I looked
into the precious eyes of my newborn, nothing could
dig me out of that hole. Not the support of my
husband, the beautiful love and support of my
family, or the tons of hugs and kisses I received from
my other two daughters. *When will it get better?*

I thought My anxiety and depression were only getting worse. I recall during an argument my husband and I were having; I can't even remember what about, but I do remember having a horrible feeling rush over me that was accompanied by sweaty prickly armpits, rapid heartbeat and terrible pain in my back that felt as if my kidneys were palpitating. What is going on with me? Is this happening again? I questioned myself because that wasn't me. My husband was concerned and asked me to speak with my doctor about what I'd been feeling, so I finally did.

A few weeks later, I scheduled an appointment to see my primary care physician. While waiting in the room to be seen, I looked down at the clipboard at what appeared to be ridiculous and personal questions, "Do you have feelings of worthlessness?" and "Do you lack interest or pleasure in doing things?" I answered honestly. So many thoughts crossed my mind in these moments. *They are going to think I'm freakin crazy* I thought, or *they are going to try to take my kids from me* was another thought that crossed my mind. *Then, when I tell them where they could go and how they could get there they will REALLY think I'm crazy and medicate me* I thought. "Ok Lord, help me" I said to myself out loud.

The doctor came in, spoke, asked me some questions, and went over the questionnaire with me. It wasn't at all like what I drummed up in my mind. Your mind can sure get away from you and take you to some deep dark corners. The next question the doctor asked me made me pause. A question that I was hesitant to answer. "Have you had any thoughts of harming yourself or your children?" *How do I answer this?* I thought. "Myself, yes, but not my kids" She started talking to me and asked me if I tried to harm myself and I told her no. As I started to cry, I thought about the times, I considered driving my truck off many bridges, or harming myself in other ways I'd rather not mention. I told her "I just feel like I don't want to be here anymore, but then I think and know that my children need me, and I want to be here for my children." My doctor was very understanding and took the time to listen. She told me that she wanted me to take an anti-depressant and anxiety medication as well as provided me with pamphlets and hotline numbers and told me to follow up with her in three weeks. After leaving the doctor's office I went to pick up the medication she'd prescribed, went home, stared at the pill bottles, and put them away in the medicine cabinet. The bottles remained there. I did not start the medication and I did not go to my three-week follow-up.

Dealing with the depression and suicidal thoughts was hard because very few people knew what I was really dealing with. Most days I put on a smiling face when all I really wanted to do was stay in bed, stay away from people, or disappear. I made the decision to forgo taking any medication and fully rely on God. So many times, I turned to the scripture that reads "The Lord himself goes before you and will be with you; he will never leave you nor forsake you. Do not be afraid; do not be discouraged." – Deuteronomy 31:8 NIV. And I know this to be true because I've made it this far, through so many obstacles, trials, and life-threatening situations that God has brought me through. God has shown me time and time again that He is there, He is real, and He is walking right beside me.

I waited patiently for the Lord; he turned to me and heard my cry. He lifted me out of the slimy pit, out of the mud and mire; he set my feet on a rock and gave me a firm place to stand. He put a new song in my mouth, a hymn of praise to our God. Many will see and fear the Lord and put their trust in him.

Psalm 40:1-3 NIV

CHAPTER 9

Adrian

It's 2014 and there I was in year two working for another Agency that didn't appreciate me or what I had to offer. Sure, some did, but not all. That's just how it goes. When I began in 2013, I started in a small customer service area that was very demanding and paid very little, but I had a plan to move to the department I really wanted to be in, that matched my background and experience and in only 2 months, the position I'd been wanting became available. Some thought I was foolish to go for a higher position that paid more in such a short amount of time, but me on the other hand, well I believed God was presenting an opportunity for me to shine and get to where I really wanted to be, and I was right! I applied for that position and was notified that I had been selected to interview before a board of members in that department. It was always a little nerve-wracking interviewing with multiple people as opposed to sitting with one person, but I went into my interview with confidence and a prayer. "What God has for me is for me, and Lord I pray this position is for me," I said to myself. A few days later when I got a call at my desk to report to the department from where I recently interviewed, I knew I had gotten the job. It was an exciting time, and I was ready to put my experience and knowledge to use and to top it off, the team was happy to have me aboard.

Not even two weeks into my new position, and life tried to bring me down. Isn't it always this way? You're sitting in bliss because of a new job or some other breakthrough and out of "nowhere" something happens to bring you back down to earth and reminds you that things aren't always perfect. I was sitting in my vehicle in the parking garage about to go home and when I put my truck in reverse it wouldn't move. I said "Lord, please don't let this be the transmission" and that's exactly what it was. Our truck had been giving telltale signs that it was having transmission issues like, making clunking noises, having a hard time changing gears and getting stuck in those gears. So low and behold, the transmission had gone out on my truck. *It's always something* I thought, but life happens. Thankfully, we had a backup vehicle at home. It was much older and very unattractive, but it drove, and I was able to drive it for two weeks while my truck was being repaired. I was also thankful that I had an understanding supervisor and manager which helped to make a stressful situation less stressful.

Not long after starting my new position, I found out that I was pregnant for the 9th time. We were actively trying for our boy so when the usual signs appeared to alert me that I might be pregnant again, it was no surprise. I purchased a pregnancy test, and it was positive so I made the call to my OB and the barrage of questions began as would the repeated early appointments and testing. The doctors and nurses were doing what was necessary to ensure the pregnancy was off to a good start, however my husband and I both had many concerns due to my history and health scares, but we both desperately wanted to try for a boy. I wanted to be able to give him the son he'd been longing for. Poor thing, he was the only guy in the house with four girls, me, and our three daughters. Even our dogs were girls, so he was outnumbered and in need of some male bonding and companionship.

With the many health scares I'd had over the years and being blessed to have more children with only one fallopian tube, my husband and I had many conversations about me having my one and only tube removed over my husband having a vasectomy. He didn't want to go down that road, although a minor day surgery we just could not agree, so we agreed to keep trying for a boy. Even though I knew it was a risk and my doctor's told me how risky it was, I wanted to have more kids. It's what I loved more than anything in this world.

My husband is the kinda guy that will wait until things get twenty times worse before going to the doctor. For example, I remember when he was working on the brakes on our vehicle one year and he came into the house and asked me to look at his eye to see if I saw anything in it. I told him I didn't, and he proceeded to rinse his eye continuously to see if that would help or if it would feel better. The next day, his eye was extremely red, grossly puffy and looked really bad. I asked him, "Honey, don't you think you should see a doctor? Do you think it was brake dust that could have fallen in your eye?" He said casually "maybe." "Really!" I said. "So, your eye has to be near falling out of your socket before you go see the doctor?" I asked him. He gave me a disapproving look. Finally, on day three of having his eye being swollen, he decided it was time to go see the eye doctor, now that it was really painful, and his vision started to become blurry. "Why did it have to get to that point? Had you gone the next day, you could have avoided this," I told him. The eye doctor had to use some tool to literally scrape the brake metal from his eyeball and do some sort of power eye wash and give him a prescription for an antibiotic. Ridiculous right? So, I should have known a vasectomy would be completely out of the question, especially when dealing with that part of his anatomy.

Once I got past the point of there being any major risks, I thought it would get easier with this being my 9th pregnancy, but it didn't. According to my physician, I have a tilted uterus which caused a lot of back pain as my son grew. I never experienced the back pain I was having with my previous pregnancies with the girls. The pain was excruciating. No matter what I did, or how I laid or positioned myself, nothing eased the pain. I tried heating pads, cold packs, stretching, warm baths, running hot water on my back while in the shower, and pushing on my stomach to get him to move around thinking maybe he would cut me some slack, but to no avail. I was also suffering from sciatica, a sharp pain that radiates along the sciatic nerve which ran down the right side of my leg from my lower back. I would often stumble when trying to stand and sometimes I couldn't even put pressure on my right foot to walk. It was debilitating at times. There were times I would literally lay on the couch almost all day curled up crying in pain.

Working during that time became very difficult and I missed a lot of days on the job. I dreaded going to work to sit in a cubicle for 8 hours in the pain I was in. Just imagine sitting in a cubicle, within a small, confined space of maybe only 7 other cubicles with not a single window to the outside. At that time nearly everything caused me pain, walking, sitting, bending, driving, hell it was even hard to breathe at that point. I just knew it was a boy that was giving me this much trouble. Even though we had a sonogram that confirmed we were having a boy but after having three girls there was still a little doubt. Sonograms have been wrong for some people many times and I was praying this would not be one of those times.

With no relief for my back pain, I began looking for other remedies and a friend of mine gave me the number to an amazing chiropractor and wellness specialist to see if there might be anything he could do to help with the pain I was having. I was a bit skeptical at first and thought to myself, n*othing, outside of having the baby, can help with this back pain.* Once arriving to see the specialist, I explained the pain I was dealing with and expressed how I didn't think there was much he could do for me because of my being pregnant. He explained there were actually a few things he could do to help and that his services might even help the baby to position himself in a way that would ease my suffering.

I was in my 8th, almost 9th month of pregnancy and Adrian was currently in a breach position. Of course, we decided to name him Adrian Jr., being the first boy. The chiropractor explained what he could do, how often I could come in, and that it may also help the baby turn. I had never been to a chiropractor or wellness specialist before, and I was intrigued and nervous at the same time. The crackle I heard from that initial neck pull freaked me out a little. Then there was the pop of what sounded like my hip cracking from a leg push technique he did next. My absolute favorite thing about going in to see that specialist was the roller massage table he placed me on at the end of my appointment. That thing was so great it made me want to buy one to have at home! Nothing hurt and most importantly, I felt like a new woman afterward. My body felt loose, relaxed, and renewed. It was amazing but it was short-lived. About a week after my appointment the back pain was back, and so was that damn sciatic pain. I knew the only cure-all would be to get Adrian Jr. out of me, and time was just not passing fast enough.

It was finally the end of December of 2014, and I prayed that boy would come before his due date of January 10th, but he was stubborn. I knew that because he was still in a breached position and laying the way he wanted to in my womb. My blood pressure started to go up, and I was still throwing up at random times during the day at that stage of my pregnancy. The vomiting got so bad that I started to lose weight and they had to prescribe a tiny dissolvable pill called Ondansetron for me to take when the nausea hit. I hadn't gained much weight and even lost a few pounds during the holiday season, so you know something was wrong with that picture. As time drew near, I began to have false labor. My doctor decided since we were close to Adrian Jr. arriving that I should be on bed rest and monitor my blood pressure and he scheduled to have me come in on January 6th to induce labor. I asked if he could do the induction on the 7th instead of the 6th, but he told me he would not be on call and another doctor would have to deliver him, but I didn't want another doctor. I really wanted him to come on his own and in hindsight, I feel like I should have let him come on his own due to the complications that would arise during his birth, but I was *soooo* ready for this to be over.

January 6th came slowly but I made it. I arrived at the hospital early that morning to get checked in. My favorite OB came in to talk to me while the nurses were getting everything set up. I was so glad I could do this while he was on duty because he made me feel really comfortable and he was a physician that really listened and genuinely cared about his patients. Even though that was my 4th birth, I was very nervous and started to worry after lying there for hours waiting for the Pitocin to kick in to help the labor along.

I always asked myself when the contractions

become unbearable *why am I doing this again?* Unfortunately, as strong as I am, I have never been strong enough to endure the pain that comes with labor. Breathing through it, meditating through it, and praying through it did not help me to deal with that level of pain. God bless all the women that can endure it without any meds. That just ain't me. My pain tolerance was very low and still is. It was finally time for the epidural. I hated that part. Bending over, doing your best to keep still all while contracting so they can stick a ridiculously long needle, to inject an anesthetic, in the space around my spinal nerves. Just the thought of it makes me cringe. I had had an epidural with my 3 prior births but this time, something was different. Not even 10 minutes after having the epidural my baby became stressed in the womb and I began to feel strange. I felt weak, queasy and I knew something wasn't right. My blood pressure started to drop, I felt itchy and tingly all over and I started to panic. My panic grew when the anesthesiologist was hanging around, nurses were coming in and out in a rush and pacing all over the place and my doctor was hanging around and speaking to the anesthesiologist. My theory is the anesthesiologist did something wrong and gave me the wrong dose, but to this day I do not know what caused my body or the baby's body to react the way it did. I was no longer dilating, and my baby was distressed, and his movement started to decline. My doctor rushed over and explained that we needed to have an emergency C-section. My heart dropped. I immediately began to cry because that was not what I wanted. As if he could read my mind, my doctor said, "I know this is not the route we wanted to take but it is what's best for you and the baby in this moment."

The doctor and the nurses began to rush around the room even more and explained to my husband and my mom what was going on and what was going to happen next. My mom stayed with the kids while my husband prepared to be in the operating room with me. Once ready I was rushed down the hall to an extremely bright white and sterile, freezing cold room. My anxiety was at 1000. I could feel my kidneys pulsating and I thought and felt as if I was going to pass out. Everything happened in what seemed like minutes. The doctor was talking a lot and preparing me for what was happening and explaining everything that was going to happen next, and it all felt like a really bad dream that I could not wake up from.

While being prepped for the emergency C-section, after my husband was dressed in scrubs and a hair covering, he was right there by my side holding my hand. I've seen that look on his face before and it made me nervous. I could feel myself slipping in and out of consciousness as I heard Adrian saying my name repeatedly as if he were checking that I was still awake and alive to respond. In the midst of his fear of what was happening I'd hear him speaking words of encouragement, telling me I was going to be okay, while also asking the doctor and nurses what was happening. At one point I felt as though I had dozed off and heard a flatline then saw a nurse put something in my IV, then immediately heard the sound of a strong heartbeat on the monitor. It was as if they were giving me something to keep me alive. In what felt like semi-consciousness I just prayed, "Lord, please don't let me die." And I know God was in that room.

There it is! The sound I'd been waiting for. The cry of my healthy baby boy. *Finally, a boy*! The excitement on my husband's face was priceless. He finally had his boy. Not only was he excited Jr. was here but he was more excited to hold him in his arms. I watched in amazement from across the room while waiting to be stitched up, eyes heavy, nauseous, and throwing up while on the table, I just wanted to be rid of everything they pumped in my body so I could have a clear mind and hold my baby boy.

After being wheeled back to the birthing room, my mom was there waiting with the girls. The look on her face was of pure concern, worry, and faithful prayer all in one. She came over to me, kissed me, and asked me how I was feeling. I could only respond in mumbles and moans as I came down from whatever high I was on, and it was not euphoric. I could feel I was definitely not myself. I felt like I couldn't think or talk straight. The nurses had placed those big massaging wraps on my calves to help reduce the chance of getting blood clots. It was scary to think that could happen to me. So many women, especially black women, did not make it through childbirth and the issue of black maternity mortality rate was and still is a huge concern.

It frightened me that I could be among the many women who have lost their lives after childbirth. The thought of me making it out of that hospital alive and wondering where my son was kept swirling around in my head. My mother-in-law came in to see about me but was the only one who found humor in my stupor as she laughed at how "tore up" she thought I looked. Her words, not mine. She obviously did not understand the severity of the situation. As she continued to joke, I could hear my husband say, "Come on momma," as to say that's not cool and to cut it out. After what felt like a few hours I started to come to just a little more but not enough. I felt so woozy and just downright drugged. *This can't be normal,* I thought. I did not begin to feel like myself until the next day.

This was the longest hospital stay I had had after having a child. I really did not expect to be there for five days but was told it was necessary to make sure everything was good with me and the baby and that we had no complications. There was some struggle with Adrian latching and nursing but thankfully after a week of being home, he was feeding like a pro and started gaining weight in no time.

During our hospital stay Adrian Jr. had to undergo several hearing tests and we were told he was not responding normally to the hearing screenings. The nurses and my OB explained that it was pretty normal due to being birthed by C-Section and not Vaginally. It was explained to us that babies born by C-section were more likely to fail their hearing tests because babies that are born vaginally are born with a force that helps with clearing middle ear fluid. That was my first time hearing or experiencing such a thing and I thought it was interesting to say the least. Once we took Adrian Jr. to his first newborn appointment with the pediatrician, he was tested again and "passed with flying colors" they said. But to this day I still think he has hearing issues. Not really, it's just selective hearing when his mom and dad are calling him; like most kids have.

We are hard pressed on every side, but not crushed; perplexed, but not in despair; persecuted, but not abandoned; struck down, but not destroyed.

2 Corinthians 4:8-9 NIV

CHAPTER 10

The 6th

The time had come for me to leave another State job. I'd accepted a higher-paying position at yet another State agency and was finally happy where I landed. My boss was great, my coworkers were great, well, most of them, but more importantly we had a director that was an incredible leader and set the tone for what a supportive agency and work family should look like. I actually enjoyed my time there very much but still wasn't sure it was where I truly belonged. See, although I was happy, I still didn't feel completely fulfilled. After all, I never had plans to sit behind a cubicle for most of my life. I wanted more for myself and for my family. My dream has always been to own my own business, make my own schedule and provide a life for my family that would allow us to travel, be financially free and enjoy life.

One day while sitting in my cube, something just

didn't feel right. I had this overwhelming feeling come over me. I felt as if something was happening to me or that something was about to happen. I literally stopped what I was doing, and just sat there listening to my thoughts and tried to hear God speak. I was about 3 to 5 days late from getting my period and thought *oh no, I'm pregnant and something is wrong.* I didn't really think much of my cycle being 3 to 5 days late because my hormones were all over the place and my cycle was not consistent. I've been late for a week before and wasn't pregnant, so 3 days didn't worry me. But have you ever just gotten a strong feeling in your gut to where you just know that you know you are right about something? Well, this was one of those times for me. I decided to run into Walmart on my way home before picking up the kids from daycare and school. "I'm pregnant, I just know I am," I said to myself. I wanted to take the test as soon as I walked in the door, but I had to get the kids settled, start dinner, and get them started on their homework. Finally, when everyone started to wind down after their baths and were getting ready for bed, I took the pregnancy test, and I was right, it was positive. I knew what I needed to do.

The next morning right at 8 o'clock, I called my OB and told them I had taken a pregnancy test and because of my extensive history, I already knew the drill and what was next. "I'm sure you knew what I was going to say next by now as well." The nurse asked me to come in to have blood work and a quantitative test done so they could see the hormone levels which would tell them whether I was having a good pregnancy or not. The higher the levels, the higher the chance of a good pregnancy. I was already preparing myself to get ready to be on meds to help with my lack of progesterone.

After going to the doctor's office, the next morning to have blood work done, while walking back to my car, I had this sinking feeling in my stomach. A feeling that this was not a "good" pregnancy and that I was going to miscarry. It was as if God was trying to prepare me and give me the courage to face it. The courage I never had before. Not that I was being negative or hoping for a miscarriage, but believe it or not, it was a feeling that

God was speaking to me and telling me this pregnancy will be a failed pregnancy but not to worry. I literally felt comfort and knew that God was in control and telling me that even though I was going to have a miscarriage, that I should not worry, so I didn't. Because God had already told me things were going to be okay, I believed that and continued moving forward. I didn't worry. I expected the nurse to call me with results that would not be pleasing and for the numbers to be low, and that's exactly what happened. And not because I was thinking negatively, or manifested a miscarriage, it happened because it needed to happen. It happened for me and not to me because God had other plans.

The next morning, I received a call from the nurse telling me the doctor had gone over my results and wants me to come back in for another blood test in a few days, this way they could be more certain about my numbers, so I did. Again, I went in already knowing what the results would be and I was okay with it. I was comforted by knowing I had no reason to fear anything in that moment because God had strengthened and prepared me, and He was with me every step of the way. Later that afternoon the nurse called back and told me the numbers were decreasing, which were signs of a failed pregnancy. She also explained that some mild cramping and spotting would be normal and informed me of what to look out for if things took a turn for the worse. The nurse let me know that my OB would like to see me the following week to follow up and make sure things were okay and that I had safely miscarried.

This was one miscarriage I looked at differently. Because I had the courage to face what was happening and because God is faithful, I thought it was amazing how my body was ridding itself of the pregnancy. Yes, the science behind it all is amazing but the God behind it is even more so to be praised. I also thought that everything happens for a reason and that this may not be the last time I'd be pregnant. With everything that's happened, you'd think I would have my one and only tube removed or tied, or something, but I just wasn't ready to go in for yet another surgery or procedure and was told by my physician that it would be best if I didn't because of everything my body had already been through, so I remained faithful.

During this time while waiting for my HCG count to lower, I had mild cramping, and there was some bleeding, but no serious pain. This was the 6th child I had lost. Yes, it was another loss, but as I said before, this loss was different and part of a bigger blessing to come. Sure, I was a little sad and my family and co-workers who knew were sad for me that this had happened yet again, but I was comforted to know that I was losing the baby the way that I was and that it was happening the way it needed to.

I know what you're thinking. How in the world could you be comforted in having a miscarriage and losing a child, but has it ever occurred to you that God has a greater plan and is potentially keeping you from hurt, harm, danger, or disappointment? Jeremiah 29:11 says, "For I know the plans I have for you, declares the Lord, plans to prosper you and not to harm you, plans to give you hope and a future." and you have to believe that. You must look at the bigger picture. There are so many things that can go wrong in a pregnancy and giving birth, especially over the age of 35. But when you trust in the Lord and let Him direct your path, you open yourself to greater possibilities and promises that the Lord said He would fulfill. God was with me every step of the way affirming faith and promise in my loss, and that's because He had a greater plan, one that I didn't see coming, and I believed that with all my heart. I cannot say that enough.

"Therefore, since we have been justified by faith, we have peace with God through our Lord Jesus Christ, through whom we have gained access by faith into this grace in which we now stand. And we boast in the hope of the glory of God. Not only so, but we also glory in our sufferings, because we know that suffering produces perseverance; perseverance, character; and character, hope. And hope does not put us to shame, because God's love has been poured out into our hearts through the Holy Spirit, who has been given to us."

Romans 5:1-5 NIV

CHAPTER 11

Amir

Winter of 2017, there I was again in that familiar aisle in Walmart staring at the pregnancy tests and wondering which one to buy. I don't know why it was such a hard decision. As many pregnancy tests that I've purchased over the years, you'd think I'd just go grab the first one I saw off the shelf and go on about my day, but I guess it was all the thoughts swirling in my mind that had me stuck standing there. A part of me couldn't believe I was pregnant again. A part of me disliked my husband for not manning up and having a vasectomy. And a part of me wondered if it would be another girl or a boy this time. But the strongest voice in me knew it would be a fulfilled pregnancy this last time. Oh, it would be the last time. I was going to make sure that my Ob removed my only good tube so that I couldn't get pregnant again. Might as well since I'd have to have another C-section. I had always heard that once you have a C-section you could have what they call a VBAC which refers to delivering a baby vaginally after having a previous Cesarean (C-Section). But I had also heard that once you have a C-Section, it's just best to have another.

Here I am getting ahead of myself. I hadn't even taken the pregnancy test yet and there I was planning it all out in my head. Oh, and I've learned that no matter how you try to plan for things to go a certain way, there are no guarantees, but I also learned that if you ask and believe it to be so, it can and will happen. Therefore, even before the doctor could confirm that this pregnancy, my 11th pregnancy, would be a good pregnancy, I knew it would be and spoke over myself and my unborn baby that all would be well. I knew that this baby would be just fine, especially after having that miscarriage some months back where God spoke to me and told me there was a reason and that He had a plan. After getting home and taking the pregnancy test, I remember walking into Ariah's room to tell her the news. I guess just by the look on my face she could tell without me even saying a word. "You're pregnant!" she said. She kind of yelled it but just at the right octave not to be yelling at her mother. "Yessss" I told her, in a long-drawn-out kind of way that sounded like I knew I was in trouble even though I am the mother. She has a mothering way about her still to this day. I've always felt a little bad for her that she did not have any siblings closer in age and also a little guilty that I couldn't give that to her. Even though I could tell by the disappointment on her face and the occasional eye roll that she was frustrated in that moment, I knew she loved being a big sister and would love this next baby and spoil him or her the same way she did the others.

As the stick sat on the counter, there were definitely two blue lines confirming what I already knew to be true, I was pregnant again. Every now and then those toxic thoughts would creep into my mind. The dark suppressant whispers screamed silently telling me I couldn't do this, and this one wouldn't make it. I immediately drowned those thoughts with prayer, and the reminder of God's promise that I shall have the desires of my heart and I knew that I could, and I would have this child because He said it would be so. Without even knowing what my doctor would tell me, I just knew. He did it before, and He would do it again.

The next morning, I called my OBGYN to let them know that I had taken a home pregnancy test the night before and that I would like to come in for a confirmed test and because of my history I wanted to come in as soon as possible. "Sounds like a broken record by now, right?" On the day of my appointment, I wasn't nervous like the times before, I actually started to get excited. I had always missed holding a tiny baby in my arms by the time my kids reached four. That's about the age when most of them stop wanting limitless hugs and kisses and want to do their own thing. During my first trimester as the numerous tests continued, my OB recommended I have a noninvasive prenatal testing test which was known as (NIPT). My doctor explained that this was not like the amniocentesis where they stick that extra-long needle through your stomach to take a sample of your amniotic fluid. She told me it would only require the drawing of my blood which was also a relief because I hated needles and didn't want to have a huge needle injected in my belly, and the biggest blessing was that this test did not pose any harm to the fetus. She also explained since my pregnancy was considered "geriatric," basically having old eggs since I was over 35, that one of the tests would be able to detect the risk of down syndrome and other chromosomal abnormalities, as well as reveal the sex of the baby. I was thrilled that I didn't have to do an amniocentesis. The only reason I was excited for this test was because I would also be able to find out the sex of my baby as early as 9 to 10 weeks.

It is amazing how far technological advances have come to help and discover things at such an early stage in pregnancy. With four children, along with my husband and I, we had a pretty full house, including the dogs but now our family was going to gain one more human which would make our perfect seven. If you remember I previously mentioned Adrian wanted 7 children and even though we would only have 5, there would still be 7 of us in our home. Seven represents the number of completion or fullness and also represents completeness throughout the bible, so in a sense our family will be complete. Seven also holds significance to me because I was born on the 7th and baptized when I was 7. The days of my cycle also used to be 7 but nowadays I never know how long flow will visit or if she will even come on time.

I was so excited when the day came for my appointment to go over the results with the doctor. It was time for the visit which would include another sonogram and the blood test results. Over the years I was accustomed to the nervousness or anxiousness I'd have as the sonographer would prepare and place the cold jelly on my growing stomach. But not this time. I eagerly anticipated the image to appear on the screen, and most importantly, could not wait to hear the little drumming sound of my baby's heartbeat. Even though this was my 11th pregnancy, I was still amazed at the growth that was occurring inside me, and how we were able to see the progress via sonogram. I'd watch as the sonographer would measure every limb and organ while we'd chat about my past and hopes for this new life to be.

My OB and the nurses knew me, my history and how much we wanted another boy and as the nurse came to the room with the results, I could see it on her face. She was just as excited as I was to find out. "You're having a boy!" she just about screamed it. Even a nurse from the other room came to congratulate me from all the commotion. I wanted to jump up and down, I was so excited that Adrian Jr. would have a little brother and buddy and I couldn't wait to get home and give the results of the test to Adrian. And thank goodness based on the test results there were no health concerns. She asked about the sex of the other siblings, and I told her "Three girls and a boy." She was genuinely excited that I was having another boy to give my current son a little brother to play with.

I left the appointment feeling really good that

day. I couldn't believe it. I was having another boy. I could not wait to share the news with my husband and kids; I knew they would be thrilled. I called my husband before I even got to the elevator. "Guess whaaaat?" I sang in a happy questioning tone. "It's a boy." he said. He already knew! He said he'd had a gut feeling it would be. I was happy no matter what the outcome. I just wanted a healthy baby and a relatively smooth pregnancy, because knowing my history, and how horrible my pregnancy and birth was with Adrian Jr., I kind of expected that this one may be equally as hard as the last since I was having a boy.

Just as I suspected, the pregnancy was hard. The dreaded back pain was back. Once in my third trimester, the pain in my back had become unbearable. The constant use of heating pads at work and making a warming pillow with a long old sock filled with rice became my new norm. I despised working in my small cubicle and I hated being uncomfortable every day for those last three months. It was bad enough I had to sit in a tiny space, but I also had to get up throughout the day and walk around often to try and get some relief. I can't remember the number of times I went to visit the oh-so-wonderful chiropractor that specialized in helping pregnant women with their back pain. He was A-M-A-Z-I-N-G! One day I am going to buy that special rolling-back table to have in the comfort of my own home! I looked them up. They aren't as expensive as you would imagine.

Once again, work was becoming more and more unbearable. I dreaded getting up every morning and driving to work. I dreaded making the walk from my car to the building and sitting in a cubicle all day long. I had to do something different, I thought to myself. I had been toying with the idea of leaving the cubicle life for good. As a child, I always had a love for hair and had imagined I'd become a beautician and own my own salon. I did hair as a teenager and for as long as I could remember I loved the transformation aspect of doing someone's hair or even my own and the confidence it evokes. For many years as an adult, I even had a side hustle doing hair. A kitchen beautician as some would say. That was until I set up one of the rooms in my home like a salon. I had folding chairs, a counter with a complete marcel iron set and everything. I had also dreamt of becoming a nurse. I loved helping people and could see myself in a fast-paced environment like nursing. For a while, one of my aunts had been talking to me about joining the real estate industry. She invited me to a few meetings with her to get some insight into what she did and to get a glimpse of what being a real estate agent was all about. She held a high position at a very important agency while doing real estate on the side and I admired her strength and hustle. I was always fascinated by home architecture and remodels and watched a ton of HGTV. *How cool would it be to be able to show beautiful homes to people* I thought. I would soon find out there was much more involved than just opening a door and showing someone how many bedrooms or square feet, a home had.

While sitting at my computer at work one day, I decided to start doing more research to see what steps I would need to take to go to real estate school. After looking at different options, I discovered one school was giving a pretty nice discount on courses, so I decided to look into it more. After doing some math and calculating the cost and expenses, I wrote out a plan and printed multiple documents to support my research before presenting it to my husband. I also had to take into consideration that he would then be the one responsible for carrying us all on his insurance, which I knew would be a major cost difference since my children were covered at no additional expense through my current employer.

This is going to be tough I thought. Convincing my husband that I should quit my job after 13 years of state service, to start an entirely new career that I know nothing about and put the kids on his insurance was going to be near impossible. I first let him know my idea and that I had been talking to our aunt for some insight but for many months I gave it to God, prayed about it, wrote down a plan, then put my plans into action. When the time came to present the plan to my husband, he was completely on board. I couldn't believe it. Once I sat down with him to go over all the details and a step-by-step play of what I was planning to do and how we would do it, it just made sense and there was evidence that it could be done. All that was left to do was to verify the cost of coverage with his insurance so that he would have an idea of what additional money would be coming out of his paychecks and it was a done deal. In that moment I decided I was going to leave my secure position, with benefits and a 401k at the age of thirty-six and start a new career, a career I dreamt would provide me with the flexibility I needed for my kids and the opportunity to take my family to the next level of financial security and freedom. My aunt put it on my mind, God put it in my heart, and my husband approved, and that was all I needed to take the next steps.

When the time came to tell my boss, she looked at me like I was crazy. "Are you sure you want to do that?" she asked, "You're eight months pregnant!." She wasn't the only one that looked at me like I was losing my mind and being overcome by pregnancy brain. When I shared the news with some of my co-workers and friends, many tried to talk me out of it, many encouraged me but with a skeptical kind of encouragement, and many didn't care what I did. I had happily put in my two weeks' notice and was counting down the days on my calendar by marking them with big red x's for all to see. When God says yes, who can say no? I was excited for the next chapter of my life to begin.

It was finally time to leave my state job and do something I wanted to do. I happily enrolled in a real estate school and wasted no time between leaving my job and jumping right in. I began real estate school in September of 2017 where I would be learning all I needed to know for an entire month to pass the state exam. The school had the option to do online courses as well, but I preferred being in the classroom so I figured I could tough it out and complete a month of in-person classes and finish any remaining courses after having Amir. I thought since I'd be breastfeeding and up every night anyway, might as well study my material and do some coursework online when the time came (after I had him). My thoughts played out a lot easier than actual life, but sometimes it was the other way around. That's usually how it goes, we intensify things in our mind, especially during those shower thoughts and conversations with ourselves. If you know, you know.

There I was throwing up after enjoying a large salad. "Lord, why do I have to have morning sickness at all times of the day, throughout my entire pregnancy?" I said to myself. It was the worst. I had to take a so-called safe prescription medication again to try and curb my nausea, but it just did not work. I could not wait until October to have this baby! At my thirty-six-week doctor's visit, we discussed the plan to bring baby Amir into the world. Because my last child was born by emergency c-section, my doctor decided it would be best to do a planned c-section. She explained that it would be a very different experience than the last, and boy was she right. My due date was October 15th but she told me we could move it up a few days. I knew I didn't want to have him on my birthday because I wanted his birthday to be special and not to be shared with me, so we decided on October 10th. I liked the way that sounded. Ten-Ten. My baby will be born on Ten-Ten. I was excited to have another libra in the house. He would be my only little libra baby.

Getting up and going to class every day got harder and harder as I inched closer to my 39th week of pregnancy. The real estate math part was the worst for me because I've always hated math, it was never my strong suit. I looked forward to the free food that was provided by sponsoring speakers every day, that was the highlight for me. I remember one day in class after enjoying an amazing Asian meal provided by our sponsor, not even ten minutes went by before I was up and dashing to the lady's room, emptying my stomach of what I'd just eaten. I was so mad. I really enjoyed that lunch. "Not much longer to go," I'd repeat to myself to get me through. "Not much longer to go." I completed all of my in-person classes around the end of September.

Now it was time to prepare for Amir's arrival. It was finally here. The anticipation of meeting my little man, and last child I'd ever have was overwhelming, but not as much as my thoughts about the C-section. I arrived at the hospital around 6 am on October 10th, 2017. Once checked in, they took me to get prepped along with my husband in a large empty room where patients would normally be. There were multiple hospital beds with curtains that could divide each space if needed. It was so early and so quiet. The nurses came to get all my information and to start an IV and soon after the doctor came in to speak with me and to go over the plan. She was adamant that this would be a completely different experience than the last and that there was nothing to worry about.

My previous C-section was done at a different hospital by a different doctor, so I felt confident that this would be a different experience. I knew God was in the room, He watched over Amir as he grew in my belly, and in that moment, I prayed that He would be in the room with the doctors, by my side, and that there would be no complications. Why do we still doubt when we've done all this praying and begging of God? Faith of a mustard seed He says, and y'all know a mustard seed is tiny. Why does that little sliver of "what if" creep in? The devil will try to find any crack to squeeze in and whisper negative thoughts in your head. Block it with all your might. Yes, we are human, and we will have those moments of doubt and uncertainty, but when we do we have to remind ourselves that God is all loving, all powerful, all mighty, and that we can do all things through Him who strengthens us. Have positive affirmations. You have to positively affirm that you believe you will come out on the other side just fine. You have to positively affirm that your baby will be born in good health and spirit. Constantly affirm what you want and what you believe will be true, in anything and for anything. I believe that, and if you believe that, no one and no devil can change that.

One story I have about affirming great things takes me back to my firstborn Ariah. Ever since she was five years old, she had a love for the University of Texas (UT). We got her involved in small camps she could attend there, whether it was science, reading, basketball camps, or simply taking her to see a girls basketball game, she would always say, "I'm going to go to UT", and she believed it in her heart, and we believed it for her because that's what she desired. Sure, I thought that could change by the time she went to high school. Who knew if her goals would stay the same or if she would be offered scholarships. Well, her love for UT never changed, her dream of writing and being in journalism never changed, and even though it was a challenging journey, I don't recall her faith wavering when it came to her getting into that school. Ariah worked hard to get into an early college program that would allow her to graduate high school with an associate's degree. She worked her butt off and as a result she ranked #17 in her class of over 450 students. My baby was one of the many kids that were robbed of their grand moment of graduating with their class in 2020 due to the pandemic, but she stayed true to affirming what she wanted and what she would accomplish. Now she's a UT graduate.

While lying there on the operating table waiting

for Amir's arrival, listening to all the hustle and bustle of the nurses, the constant beeps of the machine, and the pressure pulling and tugging at my womb, it was a little nerve-wracking, but I felt a calm and a peace that I did not feel with my last c-section. *This is wayyyy better* I thought to myself. "Thank you God," I said in that moment. I remember my husband making a comment about why he should not have looked over that sheet because he saw all of my organs, all the while I'm talking to the doctor making sure she removes my only fallopian tube and asking if she can just go ahead and do a tummy tuck while she's in there. We all laughed while my husband sounded like he was about to lose his morning breakfast all over the operating room floor.

Amir was finally here. He was so tiny, only weighing 6lbs 4oz. All my babies were small, and I knew he wouldn't be any different. I also knew once my milk came in, his tiny body would quickly add on those liquid gold pounds, and he'd be a little chunkster like the rest of them. Breastfeeding my babies always gave me so much joy knowing I was giving them the very best nutrition they needed right from my body as God intended. Although the cracked nipples, plugged ducts, and mastitis were agonizing, I'd do it all again if I could.

Later that night I did a live video on social media about how Amir had made his entrance into this world and that I couldn't be happier or feel more blessed because of everything I had been through to get here and the fact that I am still here because of God's favor and love. I reminded the people watching that video of the pain and losses I'd had and shared my joy and excitement of welcoming my 2nd baby boy to this world. Many did not know all the trials, pain, tears, and heartache I endured, or the near-death experiences I'd had. Some had forgotten what it took for me to have the children I have, and some didn't even care. I said to myself, "You know what, I am truly a living testimony, and I don't need anyone's validation, approval, or acceptance because I know what God has done for me and the miracles he's performed in my life." Yes, miracles. Growing a human being in your womb is a God-given miracle.

I knew after having my rainbow baby Azriel in 2010 that I would eventually share my trials and triumphs, but I never imagined it would come to this. After many years of procrastinating and moving at a snail's pace to do what God put on my heart to do, this labor of love is finally finished.

Praise be to the God and Father of our Lord Jesus Christ, the Father of compassion and the God of all comfort, who comforts us in all our troubles, so that we can comfort those in any trouble with the comfort we ourselves receive from God. For just as we share abundantly in the sufferings of Christ, so also our comfort abounds through Christ.

2 Corinthians 1: 3-5 NIV

Epilogue

The Blessing In It All

So here I am in 2025, finally in a career I love and building other businesses with my kids. For years, I brainstormed about putting it all in a book, figuring out a title, worrying about how I'd get it published, or if I would even be able to convince people to pick it up and read it. I even beat myself up about how long it has taken me to finish this book and felt I should have been done with it sooner and even let the comments and thoughts of others get to me because I didn't know where to start or what to do exactly.

But what I do know is that God spoke to my heart a long time ago and told me I needed to share it because someone needed to hear it, and that I needed to write about all He's brought me through because it would glorify Him. No matter how long it took me, I knew He would help me do it, and that He would work in a way no one else can, to make sure this book and these tests and trials would speak to the hearts of those who needed to hear it most.

So, as I share my pain, my heartache, my suffering, and my blessings with you, I want you to know it was not all in vain. Your struggles, whatever they are, your sacrifices, whatever they are, your tears, no matter how many times you've cried, are all a part of a greater plan that you couldn't possibly imagine. Your loss, although painful, is potentially someone else's path to a freeing which is what God could have intended. Not that God wants you to suffer or be in pain, but He wants your suffering and pain to be a part of someone's healing, not just your own. God wants to get the glory and for others to realize they aren't alone in their struggles, and neither are you. You are never alone. Have you ever wondered why things are happening to you? Why are you going through whatever it is you are going through? I truly believe our experiences and struggles makes us stronger and sometimes God allows us to go through things so that we can draw closer to Him for strength and courage, but also so that our test may be a testimony to others. Deuteronomy 31:6 says, *Be strong and of good courage, do not fear nor be afraid of them; for the* LORD *your God, He is the One who goes with you. He will not leave you nor forsake you."*

This is a scripture that can be such a reminder that no matter what, you are not alone, God is with you and if you allow Him to be a part of what you are going through, and acknowledge that He is walking with you, you will be comforted. This scripture is a manifestation of sorts. Think about it. When you want to manifest something or speak something into existence what do you do? You repeat it over, and over again during the day, every day until you believe in your heart, mind, and soul that it is so. Scripture is the same. Tell yourself you are strong. Tell yourself you are courageous. Tell yourself you are not afraid. And finally, tell yourself that you know without a shadow of a doubt that God is with you and wants nothing but the best for you, then read the scriptures that help you over and over. When you manifest strength, good health, and courage, you can and will become those things. The bible says there is power in your tongue and your mind. Three scriptures that attest to this truth are:

Proverbs 18:21, Philippians 4:8 and Matthew 21:22.

Read them and make them a part of your daily affirmation routine.

Proverbs 18:21 reads: *Death and life are in the power of the tongue: and they that love it shall eat the fruit thereof.*

Philippians 4:8 reads: *Whatever things are true, whatever things are noble, whatever things are just, whatever things are pure, whatever things are lovely, whatever things are of good report, if there is any virtue and if there is anything praiseworthy—meditate on these things.*

Matthew 21:22 reads: *And whatever you ask in prayer, you will receive, if you have faith.*

And even when you try to ignore that little voice inside, there is an undeniable tugging at your heart, and your soul, urging you to share your truth, share your story, and share your pain so that it may be a blessing to those who have walked a similar path. My prayer is that you'll find that unbreakable courage to continue pressing forward and continue believing that God is there with you, and He will never leave you. I pray that you have been blessed in some way by what you've read or heard about my pain and experiences. Thank you, because you didn't have to pick up this book, but you did, and for that, I will be forever grateful.

If God carried me, He will carry you too!
God Bless You.

ABOUT THE AUTHOR

Texas Native LeTicia Rivera-Clemente, is a successful real estate agent, mentor, author, mother and wife. Her and her husband have been married for 19 years and have shared a life together for a total of 24 years. Together they have five beautiful children ages 23, 15, 13, 10, and 8.

LeTicia's upbringing and extensive background in customer service and consumer protection has fueled her passion to be there for others however she could. Her considerable work ethic and tenacity helped her leave a dead-end career in State Government in 2017 and go into business for herself as a REALTOR® and Entrepreneur.

LeTicia's goal and purpose of her debut book is to share her journey of pain and faith and to encourage others to share their stories in an effort to strengthen the faith of others.

Please be sure to check out my website www.fiveoutofeleven.com and leticiarivera-clemente.com and like and follow fiveoutofeleven on FB, Instagram and TikTok.

I encourage you to share your stories and engage. I would love to hear from you!